COMPARATIVE STUDIES IN DEMOCRATIZATION

edited by
ANDREW APPLETON
WASHINGTON STATE UNIVERSITY

A GARLAND SERIES

BEYOND THE BARRICADES

WOMEN, CIVIL SOCIETY, AND PARTICIPATION AFTER DEMOCRATIZATION IN LATIN AMERICA

TRACY FITZSIMMONS

Routledge
Taylor & Francis Group

LONDON AND NEW YORK

First published 2000 by Garland Publishing, Inc.

Published 2020 by Routledge
2 Park Square, Milton Park, Abingdon, Oxon OX14 4RN
52 Vanderbilt Avenue, New York, NY 10017

First issued in paperback 2020

*Routledge is an imprint of the Taylor & Francis Group,
an informa business*

Fitzsimmons, Tracy.
    Beyond the Barricades: women, civil society, and participation after democratization in Latin America/ Tracy Fitzsimmons
        p. cm.— (Comparative studies of democratization)
    Includes bibliographical references and index.
    ISBN 0-8153-3736-1 (alk. paper)
        1. Democratization—Chile. 2. Political participation—Chile.
3. Women in politics—Chile. 4. Democratization—Latin
America. 5. Political participation—Latin America. 6. Women in politics—Latin America. I. Title. II. Series.

JL2681 .F58 2000
320.98—dc21

                                                    00-021684

ISBN 13: 978-1-138-96457-0 (pbk)
ISBN 13: 978-0-8153-3736-2 (hbk)

Contents

Preface and Acknowledgments

Like most authors of academic works, I did not set out to do this study purely because of an unanswered theoretical question that just kept nagging at me. I arrived at it *both* inductively and deductively. The inductive portion is probably best illustrated by an experience I had while a graduate student in Chile in December 1989. As I was on a bus heading down the main thoroughfare in Santiago on my way to take an exam, the bus got stuck in the middle of the final pre-election *manifestación*, of which there had been many that autumn. To be fair, I could have gotten off the bus, hopped on the subway, and made it to the exam in plenty of time. But instead I got off the bus and joined the placard-waving, slogan-chanting crowd of thousands of pro-democracy activists. I stayed until the protest was broken up by the military wielding water-guns, tear gas and batons. Their violence sent people running in all directions and treated many — including, I saw, a pregnant woman and a young boy of about ten years old — to beatings on the street. In the years that followed I wondered, anecdotally, what had happened to the many individuals who had claimed the streets and the public eye during the political mobilizations of the fall of 1989. Where had all the protesters gone? What does life beyond the pro-democracy movement look like for those individuals and their organizations once they are in democracy? Would women be able to claim the equality that democracy had promised?

All one had to do was read the newspapers to know that the pro-democracy wave was cresting and similar political mobilizations were occurring in other parts of the world — witness Tiananmen

Square in China, Solidarity in Poland, anti-SLORC movements in Burma. Such highly publicized mobilizations coupled with my own trips to Central America in the early 1990s, when peace agreements and neo-liberalism were the central issues, continued to trigger for me this question of, what happened (or will happen) to those protesters after the barricades to democracy have been dismantled?

The deductive approach to these questions came from spending too much time hanging around institutions of higher learning, which for me translated into actually believing in (and demanding, my students would add) the importance and utility of finding the theoretical home of a question. My queries found their home — or rather the notable *lack* of one — in the juncture of democratization and organization theories. This project then matured from the aforementioned questions to become my doctoral dissertation, and now after further research and many revisions, this book. In it, I examine how the emergence of new democracies affects the organized participation of citizens. I explore the assumptions of prominent theorists that a transition to democracy paradoxically demobilizes civil society, leading to a disbanding of organizations and a decline in participation; but my findings challenge these assumptions and demonstrate that the story is more complex. First, while "political" participation lessens significantly, overall participation is not reduced. Citizens continue to participate actively in the social, economic and cultural realms following a transition to democracy. At the same time, organizations which were formerly overtly "political" and their membership remain structurally and hierarchically intact, responsive primarily to crisis situations. Despite the changed character of participation, therefore, there remains an organizational residue in the political realm. Second, feminist organizations confirm the demobilization hypothesis: while many women have left the household, their identity groups have failed to occupy the public space — or it may be that they have been co-opted out of the public space. I suggest that these findings have implications for the stability, type and quality of democracy.

But before beginning this discussion, I wish to make one clarification. This study is about the *process of moving toward* a consolidated democracy, it is not about democracy itself. However, insofar as it helps the reader, the working definition of democracy for this paper is a minimalist one; it includes competition for state offices, accountability of rulers to the ruled, civilian control over the military, the right of citizens to participate, and basic political and civic rights (see Chapter 1 for more on this). Until recently, such democracies have been a novelty in Latin America, and continue to be in many other parts of the world. While we now have many studies of democracy — and more recently the process of getting there — we still lack systematic studies of how the process affects the outcome. This project attempts such a study, but seems to have raised as many questions as it has answered.

Both the process of research and writing this book, and its outcome, have benefited from the support and advice of many colleagues and friends. In the decade I have known her, Terry Lynn Karl has never failed to be an astute teacher, a tough critic and an inspiring friend; she has influenced my research interests and my love of teaching more than anyone. Philippe Schmitter's comments on my research and writing were so thorough that nearly every paragraph in this book has benefited from his advice and wit. I was fortunate to work with Jim March before his retirement; while writing the first draft of this manuscript, no one consistently asked such insightful questions as he did. Forrest Colburn, Gillett Griffin, Paul Sigmund, and Rodolfo Stavenhagen turned me on to the study of Latin America — for that and for their continued support, I am indebted to them. Ken Roberts shared my interest in Chile, and if it had not been for his initial insight and guidance, the idea for this project would have remained just that.

Empirical data for this study was collected on several extended research trips to Chile between 1991 and 1995; because one might expect participation patterns to change or become heightened during an electoral moment, one of those research trips included the December 1993 presidential elections. I was also in Chile as a graduate student for fifteen months from July 1989 to September 1990, during which time the country was officially transitioning from authoritarian to democratic rule. Therefore, instead of just a snapshot glimpse at participation levels, I was able to observe organizing patterns over an extended period of time. The information and anecdotes in this book came from over one hundred interviews with

activists, government officials and donors, from analysis of participation patterns, from participant-observation of civil society
groups, and from archival research. While in Chile, my research
greatly benefited from the help of numerous individuals and institutions. Many thanks to the researchers, librarians and staff of the
Political Science department of the Pontifícia Universidad Católica
de Chile, FLACSO, and the Programa de Economía del Trabajo
(PET). Those at PET were particularly generous with their time and
knowledge, especially Roberto Urmeneta and Gladys Quezada. The
two of them, together with Rodrigo Godoy, Pedro Delano, Mariela
Oelckers, William de St. Aubin, Ximena Godoy, Eugenio Gigogne,
Raul and Amalia Pineda, Dino Soto, Winnie Lira, Eduardo
Rodriguez and Claudio Leal have made my time in Chile unforget-
table. I am also indebted to the individuals and organizations in
Chile who lent their time and reflections to this study.

I am grateful to the Center for Latin American Studies at
Stanford University, the Knowles Foundation, the Stanford Center
on Conflict and Negotiation, and the University of Redlands for
funding my research and writing. Because of the support and
friendship of those who have worked there, Stanford's Casa Bolívar
and the third floor of Redlands' Hall of Letters have seemed much
more like homes than academic institutions. Lynnae Pattison has
been particularly helpful in editing the manuscript; her keen eye,
and the research assistance of Katie Torrington and Tracy Hughes,
have been invaluable. In many ways, this book has been not my
project, but *our* project. Chuck Call, Sharon Lang, Keith Osajima,
Sara Schoonmaker, and Pat Wasielewski have been the core of a
very lively and helpful annual summer writing group in Redlands
and have all been great friends, critics, and motivators.

There are many other friends and colleagues whose academic
work has been an inspiration or whose friendship has been invalu-
able. They are: Bari Anhalt Erlichson, Mark Anner, Graeme Auton,
Nora Bensahel, the Besen family, Marjorie Castle, Dominique
Blom, Ron and Becky Curran, Evan Feigenbaum, Sal and Evie
Ferrandini, Elisabeth Friedman, Kris Johnson Ceva, Liz Jusino,
Sanjeev Khagram, Jutta Mohr, Barbara Morris, the Privat family, Kim
Reisler, Art Svenson, Harold Trinkunas, and the Walsh family. Most

importantly, I thank my parents, Don and Carolyn Fitzsimmons, my brother David, and Chuck Call for their loving support.

Finally, to Olga Pineda — how I wish that she had outlived Pinochet. It is to her memory, and unforgettable laugh, that I dedicate this book. As Olguita would say, *fíjate*.

Figures and Tables

Acronyms

ANEF	Asociación Nacional de Empleados Fiscales (National Association of State Administrative Workers)
CDT	Central Democrática de Trabajadores (Workers' Democratic Central)
CE	Centro de Estudiantes (Center of Students)
CEDUC	Corporación de Educación Sindical (Corporation for Union Education)
CEMA	Centros de Madres (Mother's Centers)
CODEM	Comité de Defensa de Derechos de Mujer (Committee in Defense of the Rights of Women)
CONAR	Comitée Nacional para Ayudar a los Refugiados (National Committee to Help Refugees)
COPACHI	Comité de Cooperación para la Paz en Chile (Committee of Cooperation for Peace in Chile)
CNS	Coordinador Nacional Sindical (National Union Coordinator)
CNT	Comando Nacional de Trabajadores (National Command of Workers)
CTC	Confederación de Trabajadores del Cobre (Confederation of Copper Workers)
CTCH	Central de Trabajadores de Chile (Central of Chilean Workers)

CUT	Central Unitaria de Trabajadores (Central Union of Workers)
FECH	Federación de Estudiantes de la Universidad de Chile (Federation of Students of the University of Chile)
FESECH	Federación de Estudiantes de Chile (Chilean Student's Federation)
FESOL	Feria de la Economía Solidaria (Economic Solidarity Fair)
FEUC	Federación de Estudiantes de la Universidad Católica (Federation of Students of the Catholic University)
FLACSO	Facultad Latinoamerica de Ciencias Sociales (Latin American Department of Social Sciences)
FOSIS	Fondo de Solidaridad e Inversión Social (Fund for Economic Solidarity and Social Investment)
INJ	Instituto Nacional de la Juventud (National Institute for Youth)
MEMCH	Movimiento Pro-Emancipación de la Mujer Chilena (Movement for Women's Emancipation)
MF	Movimiento Feminista (Feminist Movement)
MOMUPO	Movimiento de Mujeres Pobladoras (Women Pobladoras Movement)
MUDECHI	Mujeres de Chile (Women of Chile)
OEP	Organización Económica Popular (Popular Economic Organization)
PDC	Partido Democráta-Cristiano (Christian Democratic Party)
PC	Partido Comunista (Communist Party)
PET	Programa de Economía del Trabajo (Program on the Economics of Work)

PPD	Partido para la Democracia (Party for Democracy)
PS	Partido Socialista (Socialist Party)
PROSAN	Programa de Solidaridad de Alimentación Nacional (Solidarity Program for National Nourishment)
RN	Renovación Nacional (National Renovation Party)
SERNAM	Servicio Nacional de la Mujer (National Service for Women)
SOFOFA	Sociedad para el Fomento de Fabricación (Society to Promote Manufacturing)
UDI	Union Democrática Independiente (Independent Democratic Union)
UP	Unidad Popular (Popular Unity)

<u>Beyond the Barricades</u>
Women, Civil Society, and Participation
After Democratization in Latin America

CHAPTER ONE

Theoretical Paradoxes of Participation During and After Democratization

It is difficult to find (volunteer) members.
No one does anything.
Now under democracy, no one works for free.[1]

If he (Pinochet) couldn't stop
us (from organizing),
why should democracy stop us?[2]

Participation in organizations is about knowledge, skills, identity, and power. Beginning at a very young age — be it through a soccer club, a church, or scouts — we learn that organizations may impart skills, create friendships, respond to our needs, or prompt debate. Whether positive or negative, such participation heavily influences us and changes the way in which we interact with the world around us. Likewise, participation plays an influential role with citizens and their political system, training individuals to be leaders and providing citizens with the opportunity to affect policy decisions. This is especially true in democratic polities which emphasize the importance of "the people."

Yet contemporary theorists, in the tradition of liberal democracy, tend to leave "the people" aside and instead emphasize elites and elections. Democracy, according to Joseph Schumpeter's widely accepted definition, is "a political method...that institutional arrangement for arriving at political decisions which realizes the common good by making the people itself decide issues through the election of individuals who are to assemble in order to carry out its will" (1943: 250). Dahl (1972) and Tourraine (1988) also posit definitions of democracy that center upon competition for people's votes; their focus is almost exclusively on elite actors vying for office.

Other theorists acknowledge that democracy is much more than elections and elites. Many suggest that democracy also entails a political system where rulers are held accountable to the ruled (Schmitter, 1986), the military is held under civilian rule (Karl, 1990), the interests of the people are represented and protected (Bentham, 1882), and there exists political equality among citizens (Rousseau, 1762). Proponents of participatory democracy, such as Carole Pateman, take the definition one step further, arguing that every individual living in a democratic society should have the opportunity to participate directly in all spheres of political life (1970: 105-6). Such definitions extend the concept of democracy from the elites to the masses, and by inference, from the national to the local level.

Despite the contestation over appropriate definitions for democracy, there is general agreement that civil society matters for democracy.[3] Conventional wisdom established by Alexis de Tocqueville (1832/1956) posits that the "thickness" of civil society is essential to the establishment of durable democracies. In other words, the development of civil and political associations, and the relationships among and between them, are crucial to the livelihood of democracy. Such associations are said to serve as a system of checks and balances on government, protect the rights and interests of the citizens, and counterbalance the will of the majority. Citizens must be permitted to associate with each other through organizations so that they can attend to the small matters which governments do not have the interest nor the time to handle. De Tocqueville argues that freedom of association may need to be limited in order to assure that organized groups do not overcome the authority of the government, but the potential dangers raised by the existence of associations are preferable to their absence. Were associations to be prohibited, the tyranny of the majority would be

assured, and the concept of personal liberty would be destroyed.
Associations also help to avoid revolutions, because through them
citizens become involved in pursuits that necessitate a relatively
stable environment; when given the opportunity to choose, citizens
will opt to maintain that tranquillity instead of revolting. De
Toqueville considers the right of association to be akin to the right
of individual liberty.[4]

Citizens have the opportunity to participate in most stable or
consolidated democracies far beyond voting, and their role has
been described by theorists as anywhere from life-sustaining to
life-threatening for democratic regimes. Yet notwithstanding the
extensive work on the role of organized groups and interest associations in advanced industrialized countries, there is very little
scholarship on the role of civil society in new democracies or countries returning to democracy (re-democratization).[5] Issues of participation are key for understanding the prospects for democracy in
the developing world, and for identifying the quality, type and durability of the emerging democratic polities.

DEMOCRACY, DEVELOPMENT AND CIVIL SOCIETY

It appears that the world may be reaching the end of the fourth
wave of democratization.[6] The first wave of countries making a transition to democratic rule occurred in 1848, the second after World
War I, and the third following World War II. Notably, this fourth
wave is the first to have a worldwide impact, and also the first not
to result from an international war or conflict. The current wave of
transitions to democracy began with Portugal in 1974 and subsequently swept over first Southern Europe, then South America and
East Asia, and finally Central America and Eastern Europe.
Although reverses have been evident, there is still much optimism
that this fourth wave will yield a multitude of resilient democratic
regimes (Karl and Schmitter, 1992).[7]

Yet the undertow of authoritarianism has historically proven
too strong for many countries which have undulated between democratic and repressive regimes. This has been particularly true in
Latin America where countries such as Chile, Argentina and Brazil
have experienced pendular shifts between democratic and authori-

tarian regimes. These cases and many others are making a return visit to democracy in this contemporary wave; many wonder if democracy will "stick" this time.

Such speculation is especially important in those developing countries where political instability has aggravated levels of under-development, leading to less economic investment, higher levels of unemployment, greater opportunities for governmental corruption and fewer channels for participation. Poverty levels throughout the developing world continue to be staggering, especially in Latin America and the Caribbean where, according to the World Bank's 1997 World Development Indicators, the poorest quintile of the population receives 4.5 % of the national income, lower than any other region in the world.[8] Indeed, regional 1997 GDP growth per capita was a mere 3.6% — and just 1.8% between 1991 and 1997. The United Nations Economic Commission for Latin America and the Caribbean found 39 percent of the region's population is poor, and 17 percent essentially destitute. These inequalities translate into: 74 million people being without health care, 92 million without safe drinking water, 147 million lacking sanitation facilities, 47 million adults unable to read and 5.58 million malnourished children under the age of 5.[9] Democracy brings the hope that political stability combined with more open rule will usher in a host of goods to developing countries that may alleviate their problems; such goods may be an influx of foreign investment, debt assistance, challenges to dominant political and class powers, alternative strategies for alleviating poverty, and greater representation of the needs and interests of the people. While democracy may not fulfill such expectations, if nothing else, a transition to democracy nowadays means that a country becomes eligible for a variety of bilateral and transnational loans, grants, and in-kind donations, most of which are earmarked solely for democratic societies. Therefore, a failure of democracy in these countries not only affects their political system, but also has repercussions for their development levels as well.

What factors lead to a more stable democratic regime that may at least be able to address such expectations? When and how do citizens begin to view democracy as the most desirable form of governance? Can and do citizens participate under their new democracies? These questions are vital to identifying whether the new democracies will be more resilient and enduring than those in the past. Each, in part, can be answered by returning to de Toqueville's argument about the importance of civil society in America and examining it in the context of the developing countries currently undergoing a transition to democracy. A closer look at civil society after a transition may reveal much about the durability and future prospects for democracies that emerge from this fourth wave.

More specifically, a study of civil society in the developing world may indicate what types of democracy will take hold. Will the new democracies be inclusive or exclusive, representative or direct, centralized or decentralized? A study of civil society can pinpoint whether and which actors are represented, at what levels they participate, how they articulate demands, and through which channels the government responds. A study of this sort may also indicate whether the government is the only watchdog, or if civil society also acts as a system of checks and balances on the state and on elected leaders.

Civil society may also influence the resilience or stability of democracy. In the past, ethnic or other group or class-based conflict and economic crisis have posed strong challenges to democratic regimes. Today, in the context of structural adjustment programs that often have adverse distributive effects, do organizations exist that can meet needs or respond to emergencies, thereby alleviating pressure on the state? Are actors and organizations rigid or flexible in the face of change, whether it be an economic crisis or the rise of an opposing political party? Such questions probe whether organized groups will challenge the regime to deepen its democracy, or whether they will push too hard and force its collapse.

Finally, what occurs with and within civil society directly reflects upon the quality and type of the new regime by affecting how deeply the democracy penetrates. In this manner, organizations may challenge the dominant notions of citizenship by encouraging citizens to demand greater rights for individuals and groups under democracy. Among citizens, does the sense of responsibility for the political system reach beyond that of the right to vote? Does democracy reside only in the government, or does it extend into the community, schools and households? As I will discuss below, the question of the quality of democracy attempts to go beyond the liberal notion of democracy which emphasizes elections and elites, to also include the perspective of the theorists of participatory democracy who emphasize the role of the masses. Civil society can affect the quality of the regime by widening and deepening the democracy. Organizations have the capacity to encompass more citizens, including the most frequently disenfranchised — women, ethnic minorities, and the economically marginalized. Organizations may provide outlets for the articulation of unrepresented demands and may stimulate participation in politics or community life. Yet it is important to keep in mind that organizations under democracy are not necessarily democratic. Depending on their internal mechanisms and goals, organizations can either serve as training grounds for democratic principles or as nurseries for authoritarian tendencies.

DE-MOBILIZATION OR PARTICIPATION UNDER DEMOCRACY?

As we can see, what happens to the levels and types of citizens' participation has implications for the resilience, type and quality of democracy. Nonetheless, there has been little attention given to, and less consensus about, the effect that a transition to democracy has on the organizations of civil society. Indeed, rival hypotheses exist concerning what is desirable and what actually occurs in civil society following a transition to democracy, as well as that which occurs with the relationship between citizens' organizations and political parties.

First, some scholars such as Huntington (1968) argue that certain levels of socio-economic development serve as a stimulus for political participation. They further argue that levels of economic development are directly related to political instability; modernization brings many things, including democratization, urbanization, and industrialization. These may spur increases in socio-economic levels which often lead to higher aspirations for social and political mobility. Such aspirations combined with democratization can enhance participation within civil society and may even lead to a dramatic increase in the levels of organizing as frustrated citizens join forces to make demands on the government.[10] Whereas authoritarian regimes are explicitly designed to close channels of political participation and to suppress political mobilization, democratization opens new opportunities for the articulation of such demands. Therefore, there will be a boom in citizen participation.

For Huntington, participation is something to be feared if it occurs too swiftly without (or outside) proper channels of institutionalization. Participation can be de-stabilizing to democracy because it may exert too much pressure on the state and raise unrealistic expectations among the citizenry. Such high levels of participation may be perceived as dangerous when they exceed institutional capabilities; therefore, participation must be channeled through political parties or quelled until effective channels are created. Huntington asserts that parties have the ability to extinguish revolutionary tendencies, stabilize participation levels, and control the arenas of participation of other components of civil society.[11] He thus considers participation to be desirable only when harnessed and channeled by political parties.

Other theorists concur that participation may be dangerous for democracy under certain circumstances. Lipset and Dahl believe that those in the lower socio-economic levels possess authoritarian tendencies. Therefore, an increase in the participation levels among this group can lead to conflict and instability within a democratic society. Increased participation can also de-stabilize democracy by encouraging particularisms among citizens and distorting the public agenda in favor of specific groups. Both Dahl and Berelson view disinterest and apathy on the part of citizens as being natural and advantageous; limited participation helps to stabilize democracy "by cushioning the shock of disagreement, adjustment and change."[12] Going one step further, Sartori (1962) contends that active participation of the citizenry will likely lead to a de-stabilization of democracy, and perhaps, totalitarianism.

A second position paradoxically asserts that while participation is a "good" in itself and is not necessarily de-stabilizing to democracy, organizations do tend to become much less numerous and less political during the transition to democracy. O'Donnell and Schmitter (1986) suggest that group mobilization within civil society is initially resurrected during a transition of the political system. They argue that authoritarianism may be conducive to grassroots mobilization because it eliminates electoral competition; in the absence of parties, organizations arise to represent demands. Authoritarian rule may also serve as the catalyst for mobilization because it provides an enemy target against which to unify forces. O'Donnell and Schmitter, and others noted below, suggest that this mobilization will crest and diminish as some groups depoliticize. They contend that after the peak of a transition to democracy, there occurs a de-activation of the institutions of civil society because new factors arise which lead to markedly lower levels of participation.

In their view, what are the factors which lead to this alleged demobilization and de-politicization? To begin, democratization introduces political competition to civil society. A transition brings a return or emergence of political parties which may divide organizations along partisan lines as groups vie for access to the resources or power which parties may wield. If organizations become dependent upon parties or the state for financial or policy leadership, they may become assimilated or "co-opted" into these traditional political institutions.[13] Or, in lieu of incorporating them, political parties may instead choose to crowd out organizations by competing for their members, resources or leaders. Leadership flight can be a fatal problem for some organizations; some theorists suggest that following a transition to democracy, leaders of social movements tend to move to positions in the government or political parties (Oxhorn, 1992: 430). The organizations may then demobilize when they are left without the skills and institutional memory of those leaders.

Indeed, competition may even exist between parties or between organizations. Organizations may become divided by new issues and actors which emerge with a nascent democracy. For example, Ruth Cardoso (in Escobar and Alvarez, 1992) argues that organizations and their networks fracture because under democratization they must begin to compete for access to the state; there may be a finite number of channels through which organizations can submit their demands and needs to the state. Organizations also face increased competition for funding. After a transition many international donors focus their support[14] on other countries; for example, the aid that once was destined for Argentine organizations may now be funneled to Eastern European or Balkan associations. Groups then compete not only for power, but also for scarce resources and funding.

Another factor in the de-mobilization argument is that for many organizations, a transition to democracy signals the attainment of their goal: the end of authoritarianism. Organizations are created for a purpose. Once their specified goals are attained, the organizations' *raison d'être* disappears. For example, Jane Jaquette contends that

> Successful social movements inevitably lose their reason for being, for the goal of the movement is to challenge political and social institutions and to change attitudes and behaviors. As change occurs, the energy of the movement dissipates, and the maintenance of new values and structures becomes institutionalized. (Jaquette, 1989: 194)

It is argued that after democratization, groups find it difficult to change their focus and adopt new goals. Without a clear and compelling goal, organizations can easily lose their funding and members.

Finally, government policies may be aimed at curbing mobilization. According to Canel (in Escobar and Alvarez, 1992), in pacted transitions[15] elites may attempt to minimize alternative channels of participation and thereby reduce opportunities for collective action.[16] Such policies may arise out of a Huntingtonian fear on the part of elites that increased participation among the masses will de-stabilize an emergent regime;[17] in this way, while opposition organizing is not overtly silenced, it is discouraged or made difficult.

There is a third hypothesis about what is desirable and what actually happens with participation after a transition to democracy: participation is normatively good, is not de-stabilizing, and if given the opportunity, citizens will and do participate under a democracy.

This third position does not differentiate between consolidated and unconsolidated democracies. Rousseau (1762/1968), for example, asserts that democracies are, and should be, participative.[18] He argues that once a participatory democratic system is established, it becomes self-sustaining because the process of self-government develops participative qualities in the citizens. Citizens will continue to be involved through organizations because of the psychological effects and educational benefits they receive. Citizens will also value the skills they learn and the bonds they forge. At the heart of this argument is that every citizen should have not only the right, but also the opportunity to participate in a democratic system; and once presented with the occasion, they will take advantage of it. Rousseau, along with Pateman (1970) and others, contends that active citizenship, and therefore participation, is good and should be encouraged from the household to national politics.

In contrast to other scholars of democracy, these theorists believe that participation can be both a stabilizing and bolstering force for established democracies. Pateman writes, "If those who come newly into the political arena have been previously educated for it then their participation will pose no dangers to the stability of the system" (1970: 105). Citizens who have a stake in their political system will protect it. Valenzuela (1990: 13) suggests that the more citizens participate through an organized civil society, the more secure they are, the more democratic skills they gain, and the stronger is their commitment to a democratic environment.[19] This argument assumes a great deal of citizen consciousness. When citizens value democracy, they will take great measures to assure that they do not endanger it by pushing too hard; instead, they will attempt to meet their own needs or to present their demands through channels which are not threatening to democracy. As Rousseau argues, participation also allows collective decisions to be accepted more easily by the individual; although a citizen may not support a government decision or action, they are unlikely to object or rebel because they know they were part of the decision-making process, and the outcome is a reflection of the general will. For the theorists of participatory democracy, such as Rousseau, J. S. Mill and Pateman, there is no special problem about the stability of a participatory system.[20]

What the debate on desirability boils down to is, increasing one aspect of the quality of democracy through full participation versus increasing the stability of democracy by harnessing participation. But is there really a trade-off between stability and quality of democracy? Can one not enhance the other? These questions will be explored in the ensuing chapters.

In summary, there are thus several contradictory arguments about the role, extent, and desirability of organized participation after a transition to democracy.[21] First, some hypothesize that democratization may enhance mobilization by reducing coercive constraints and by opening new channels for articulation and representation of interests. A regime change towards democracy leads to a boom in political participation, activity and demands. Yet full participation of the citizenry may be dangerous and de-stabilizing for democracy; therefore, some theorists argue that participation must be channeled through political parties in order to assure that demands of the citizenry do not exceed the institutional capabilities of the state. Second, democratization may lead to a demobilization of civil society due to shifting organizational energies and fragmenting social movements. Many of the previously existing organizations may de-politicize and their members may stop participating. While participation may be considered to be normatively desirable, it often does not exist under democracy. Finally, others hypothesize that full participation is an important and stabilizing ingredient for democracy. They contend that high levels of participation are both desirable and possible, without endangering the democracy. There are thus at least three theoretical projections concerning participation after a transition to democracy. Yet which is correct? A further exploration of democratization literature, when combined with the insights of organizations theory, sheds light on these issues.

A VIEW OF POST-TRANSITION CIVIL SOCIETY FROM THE PERSPECTIVE OF DEMOCRATIZATION LITERATURE

Despite some dissension between theorists, democratization literature[22] makes several important contributions to the study of post-transition civil society. Perhaps most significantly, it helps us to understand the environment in which organizations must interact

— in this case, a transition to a democratic regime which includes high levels of uncertainty, changing opportunities for participation, different actors, and new modes of access to power. This body of literature also helps us to recognize the unique and potentially pivotal role of political parties during democratization. Through the initial period of political liberalization, parties often take a backseat to social movement organizations. But with the advent of elections, parties and other factions of political society step into the limelight. What candidates they choose and which coalitions they form will have a great impact on the representation of citizens' interests. Likewise, whether parties incorporate, crowd out, or support citizens' organizations will have repercussions on the structure of civil society. Finally, theorists of democratization explore the complementary issues of citizenship and civil society (see Connolly 1987; Melucci 1988; Munck 1990). Types and levels of participation are directly correlated with the bonds between citizens and their country. As individuals acting within organizations affect changes, challenge traditions and propose alternative solutions in the political realm, they close the gap between citizens and the state. A more dense and participative civil society may translate into a more active and intimate notion of citizenship, which can elevate the expectations of the obligations and rights of citizens, motivate citizens to organize, as well as broaden the channels of representation.

But the democratization literature makes some broad assumptions related to civil society that may not be empirically valid. For example, Canel (1992), Pridham (1993), and O'Donnell and Schmitter (1986), in stating that political parties tend to become more visible and influential after a transition to democracy, also assume that parties begin to subsume other organizations, or that the organizations disappear or decline in their political role. In fact, the power of parties may be relegated largely to the realm of national electoral politics, leaving most organizations in local politics or civil society unaffected. Furthermore, while the rise of parties and the changing rules of the political game may indeed cause some groups to fold or integrate themselves into a government ministry or a political party, organizations may anticipate the changes and adapt accordingly. As their environment transforms, so might they. This is a possibility not recognized by democratization theorists. Finally, the strength of democratization literature — its focus on the political environment — is also its weakness. Scholars place too much emphasis on the regime level, and on the power of the state and on political parties. But the political environment is not the sole, nor even necessarily the most important, variable in the construction of a vibrant civil society. In fact, democratization literature has a gaping hole. Theorists often fail to refer to the organizations and individuals which comprise that society, as well as the economic and social domains, thereby leaving little room for actor choice or organizational adaptation.

POST-TRANSITION CIVIL SOCIETY FROM THE VIEWPOINT OF ORGANIZATION THEORY

This gap in democratization literature can be filled by turning to organization theory. Whereas the strength of the democratization literature is its focus on the specific environment, organization theory is most useful for its emphasis on the internal mechanisms of organizations, their domains, and issues. Although it has not been applied to post-transition civil society, a transition to democracy is a type of environmental change[23], and this is addressed by organization theorists.

Yet just as in the democratization literature, there is disagreement in the organization theory literature relating to this topic. On the one hand, organizations may be seen as changing infrequently; they are prone to inertia. Scholars like Hannan and Freeman (1989) posit that after organizations have been founded, they are faced with several possible trajectories: expand as is, take on another form, merge with another organization, or disappear entirely.[24] During periods of "political crisis and transformation" there is an increase in the founding and building of organizations; groups grow rapidly in number, as do their memberships. This occurs within civil society during a transition to democracy. But these theorists would concur with O'Donnell and Schmitter that such mobilization reaches a threshold after the peak of the environmental change (or in this case, the political transition) and then significantly diminishes. The assumption is that new mobilization will stagnate, and organizations will tend to merge with other groups, stagnate, or disband.

Their argument is three-fold. First, a very large number of recent foundings or "births" of organizations exhausts the supply of resources needed to build new organizations (Hannan and Freeman, 1989: 205). Potential financing, material resources, members, and political space are limited. New organizations may find it difficult to enter the playing field if it is already crowded or if resource supplies are low; competition may thus be high among groups trying to enter the field as well as among those trying to survive within it. For those organizations already functioning, some resources (such as international funding) have a finite lifetime and will dry up. This can lead to the disappearance of an organization, or it can force the organization to link up with those who have substantial resources, such as political parties or the state. Second, periods of numerous organizational foundings will tend to be followed by periods of high rates of disbandings. This is due to the presence of many youthful, or new, organizations (Hannan and Freeman, 1989: 279). It is more common for young organizations to disband because they have not built up a reserve of members, routines, leadership experience and external support. Finally, when a political crisis or transformation occurs, the environment in which an organization exists may be significantly altered. Networks, resources, supplies, and membership pools may be affected; what were once considered to be organizational goals may be met or invalidated. If organizations do not react to these changes, they may cease to exist. Hannan and Freeman (1989: 67-9) assert that most do not adapt to the changing environment because of internal and external pressures towards inertia. For example, patterns of leadership, information gathering and decision-making which have been fixed over long periods of time may make it difficult for organizations to respond rapidly to changes. In fact, in a system where information is imperfect or unavailable, an organization may not be able to judge correctly the direction of the environmental transition. Therefore, they would not be able to change accordingly. Due to such pressures, organizations may disband instead of adapting to their new environment. However, these theorists err in assuming fixed preferences of leaders and organizations. This is problematic because it portrays organizations as inflexible; and because environments frequently change, it relegates organizations to an inevitable death. Others suggest that organizations will indeed adapt to such transitions, although it may necessitate some dramatic changes in the organization or its goals. One such change is the transformation from a "value-implementing agency to a recreation facility" (Messinger, 1955: 10). Messinger claims that organizations will change their functions, but not necessarily their missions or *raisons d'être*. His case study of the Townsend Movement in the United States details the three stages of organizational transformation (see Messinger, 1955; 5-10). As the environment and membership change, there is first a deflection away from the central goals. Then membership and funding levels begin to decrease, and the organization must resort to the selling of goods — unrelated to the original mission — to finance itself. Finally, these goods will attract new members to the organization who are not committed to the former goals; without a consensus on goals, the organization will transform into a recreation facility.[25]

Other theorists submit that organizations can adapt successfully to a political crisis or transition without such a dramatic organizational change as experienced by the Townsend Movement. March (1982) portrays organizations as flexible and imaginative, arguing that changes in organizations occur because organizations and their members are responsive to their environment. He claims,

> What we call organizational change is an ecology of concurrent responses in various parts of an organization to various interconnected parts of the environment. If the environment changes rapidly, so will the responses of stable organizations; change driven by such shifts will be dramatic if shifts in the environment are large. (March, 1988: 169)

Organizations may even anticipate environmental changes and react in advance. This may be because the organization has learned from its past experience, it may have learned from the experiences of other organizations, or it may be that it correctly read the political and economic indicators signaling an imminent environmental change. Many organizations are well-prepared for such times of transition. March depicts organizations as "garbage cans," which are collections of choices looking for problems, decision-makers hunting for work, and solutions searching for issues (March, 1988: 296). Organizations are thus repositories for crisis management tools, and as such, are well-equipped to handle changes in the environment.

There are many cases of successful organizational transformation documented in the United States and Europe, although little work has been done in the field on developing countries. In adapting to environmental changes, some groups lose a sense of mission (i.e. the Townsend Movement as discussed above), others displace their goals in favor of new ones (the Women's Christian Temperance Union), and still others modify their goals without narrowing them (the YMCA). One such example of organizational transformation is the Women's Christian Temperance Union (WCTU), which was founded in the late 1800s. As outlined by Gusfield (1955), it first focused on humanitarian issues such as poverty and social services. Around 1900 it changed to emphasize temperance as the solution to the problems of the lower-classes. Then after the repeal of prohibition laws, it transformed once again, this time to proclaim their moral indignation toward the upper-middle class. Despite numerous fluctuations in the environment, the organization was able to adapt, and to do so without negatively affecting its membership levels. The Young Men's Christian Association (YMCA) also transformed its mission from religious proselytization to "character development" (see Zald and Denton, 1963). The YMCA chose to modify its goals according to changing public demands, whereas the YWCA attempted to change the interests of the public. Zald and Denton attribute the success[26] of the YMCA to the fact that it attempts to adapt to the environment, not change it (1955: 220-1). The YMCA has been able to adapt because it: 1) is not tied to one membership group, 2) is decentralized in structure, 3) is closely tied to the local level, and 4) has broadly defined goals and rules.[27]

Organization theory can also help us to clarify the relationship between an organization and its members, and the interactions between organizations; more recent work in the field sheds light on the interplay between networks of organizations. However, although the literature does address organizations within the political system, it is not especially helpful concerning the relationship between organizations and the political system. Some readers will undoubtedly point out that organization theorists address the "environment," which is said to include the political system. Yet it is hard to deny that such a catch-all term neglects the distinctive characteristics of particular political systems. Without an understanding of the nuances of democratization, organization theory will have a difficult time projecting the big picture — the effect of a transition to democracy on civil society.

Taken alone, democratization theorists and organization theorists have trouble providing an accurate depiction of civil society after a transition. Neither the effect of a transition on civil society, nor the effect of civil society on consolidation, can be grasped without combining several approaches. The democratization literature shapes the macro-picture: the environment, or in this case, the regime. Organization theory provides us the micro-picture: the unit, or more specifically, the organizations. *Organizational trajectories after democratization can only be understood by blending organization theory and the literature on democratization.* An effort of this sort helps in the specification of different paths of participation.

PATHS OF PARTICIPATION

When a country undergoes a consolidation of democracy, what path does civil society undertake?[28] As we have seen in the previous sections of this chapter, democratization theorists limit their discussions to two outcomes for civil society after a transition to democracy: organizations will either mobilize (Huntington), or de-mobilize (O'Donnell and Schmitter). But it is insufficient to look solely at these two options when analyzing the effect of democratization on the organizations of civil society. Mobilization, or what I will henceforth refer to as *continuation*, and *de-mobilization* are only two of four possible paths.[29] Continuation and de-mobilization represent, respectively, an increase or decrease in the number of participants and activities corresponding to each organization, as well as the total number of organizations in existence.

Yet focusing the debate around these two options neglects a crucial factor: organization theorists suggest that groups may adapt to changes in their environment. Such changes may be reflected in the organizations' autonomy and focus. After a transition to democracy, organizations may undergo a process of *incorporation* into the formal, government structure of the new regime or into a branch of a political party.[30] Such incorporation may be political and/or economic in nature and reflects a decline in an organization's autonomy. Incorporation corresponds to the normative preference of Huntington when he warns that political participation should be institutionalized, preferably through parties, so as not to generate instability. Incorporation was also one of the paths predicted by O'Donnell and Schmitter.

The other potential path is that groups may experience a *transformation* into a different type of organization with a distinct focus; such organizations would retain their autonomy and previous levels of mobilization. This path corresponds to March's depiction of organizations as being flexible and imaginative, and able to adapt to environmental changes. Transformation or continuation would be the most desirable paths from the viewpoint of theorists of participatory democracy. These four paths approximate and build upon Hannan and Freeman's (1989) four organizational trajectories: organizations may expand as is (continuation), take on another form (transformation), merge with another organization (incorporation), or disappear entirely (demobilization).

I suggest that there are three key factors that affect which path an organization takes after a transition to democracy[31]: *funding, leadership choices,* and *organizational target.* The first is the source and amount of *funding* an organization receives; sources may range from the state and state agencies, to political parties, to international non-governmental organizations. When the majority of an organization's funds come from one outside source, the organization may begin to lose its autonomy and undergo a process of incorporation.[32] Organizations that become economically self-sufficient may avoid this path. On the other hand, if not recuperated through other means, a dramatic decrease in an organization's funding may lead the group to disband.[33]

Choices of leadership refers to whether the leaders of an organization leave the group or stay and continue their work beyond the transition period. Leadership choices range from staying with the group, to leaving to join another institution or the government, or opting to retire to work in another field. Where a leader leaves an organization to work for the government or a political party, the organization will tend to become more incorporated into that institution's structure; or without their long-time leaders, some organizations may disband. Only those who have trained potential leaders to take the helm will avoid these paths.

Organizational target is a group's focal point, which may range from an emphasis on national level politics and regime type to local politics. In order for an organization to survive, its focus must reflect environmental trends. In many transitions to democracy, one crucial issue is the extent to which political power is devolved onto local units during the emergence and consolidation of democracy. In Latin America, this process of transferring power from the historically strong executive branch to the local governments (municipalities) is known as municipalization. Municipalization may cause a transformation in the target of an organization from national to local level issues; or, if organizations choose to ignore the trend, they may disband.

A FRAMEWORK FOR THE STUDY OF POST-TRANSITION CIVIL SOCIETY

What determines which path the majority of organizations take? What does the outcome of different paths imply for the composition of civil society? How do different paths affect the type, quality and stability of democracy? Transitions are periods of uncertainty, in which the rules and norms are unclear. When the transition is one of political systems, the rules concerning participation, access to power, and representation are initially unknown.[34] Organization theory suggest that organizations deal with uncertainty in several ways: buffering (absorbing environmental fluctuations), leveling (reducing fluctuations in the environment), adaptation (altering organization to match anticipated fluctuations), and rationing (allocating of resources or energies).[35] Democratization theorists argue that organizations de-politicize and de-mobilize after peak periods of uncertainty as the electoral process and rules of interest politics take hold.[36] Both are correct to some extent.

This book argues that *after the peak of a transition to democracy, there will likely be a temporary bajón (lessening) in participation.* There is, of necessity, an adjustment period for organizations. As suggested by democratization theorists a *bajón* occurs due to a retreat of funding, leadership flight, disagreement about the appropriate target, and confusion over rules and legal requirements. Those that were really just free-rider organizations and participants will drop out. Furthermore, after the disappearance of a common, unifying enemy, conflict of interests may result among organizations; such competition may also lead to disbanding of the weaker groups. This is particularly true after a transition to democracy when parties, not citizens' organizations, are on center stage. This *bajón* is often confused with a de-mobilization.

As *long as the transition is not reversed, such a bajón is temporary and necessary while organizations adjust to the changing political climate.* Rojas (1989) argues that it is not that groups disappear, but instead they are just re-evaluating the changing situation, making new contacts, and learning how to cope and maneuver in the new system. *Following this initial bajón or learning period, organizations then stabilize and often re-mobilize.* This argument is akin to Sidney Tarrow's (1991: 53) discussion of what he terms the "descending phase of cycles".[37] It is important to remember that organizations emerge and continue for different reasons. They may emerge to combat hunger, protest the dictatorship, defend women's rights, or supplement income levels. They may continue for reasons of identity, habit, sense of community, or enhancement of personal skills and education.

How do civil society groups continue? Because organizations are adaptable bodies. Why do organizations adapt? Because they are structurally able to adapt, and desire to do so in order to survive. Many groups are founded with a particular set of goals in mind; yet their primary goal often transforms into one of survival. Participants build organizations which can adapt when necessary to maintain themselves; organizations are constructed with mechanisms to negotiate, share power, and defend their territory or constituency. In order to adapt to a changing environment, organizations need not predict the change nor necessarily respond swiftly. The rate of adaptation need only be comparable or faster than the rate of change of the environment in order for an organization to survive. Organizations may accomplish this by learning from their past experience, through diffusion of knowledge from other organizations which have undergone a similar transition, or by carefully studying the signals emanating from the environment.

I have proposed that organizations are able and willing to adapt to a changing environment, but on which path can we expect them to proceed? *Theoretically, after a transition back to democracy most organizations will follow the fourth path of transformation.* This is particularly likely in those transitions in which power becomes less centralized, because when the political system undergoes a transition, there should occur a parallel transition of organizations within that system. As March explains, changes in organizations reflect the political, social, economic and demographic forces of the environment (1988: 167). When the environment transforms, so too, may the organizations. I argue that organizations transform in the following ways:

ORGANIZATIONAL TRANSFORMATION		
National	====>	*Local Level*
Universalistic	====>	*Particularistic*
Highly Politicized	====>	*De-Politicized*
Goal Oriented	====>	*Domain Oriented*

National to Local Level

Under an authoritarian regime, political power is centralized in the hands of a dictator or a governing junta. To varying degrees, democratization may bring a decentralization of that power. Systems that remain highly centralized force organizations to compete in a single national arena. In such cases, many organizations may be forced to disband. However, where power is devolved onto the local level, organizations may mirror that change (whereas political parties must split their energies and resources between local and national elections). In many Latin American countries, political power is becoming decentralized toward the local governments in a process known as municipalization.[38] Organizations may parallel this process because at the municipal level they are better able to affect political decisions. They also may be able to receive funding, resources, and meeting space in many municipalities — this is very important for the many organizations that relied upon international solidarity support during authoritarian rule; with the advent of democratic rule, much of that support is reallocated to other countries. National networks diminish as organizations become more isolated in their communities.

Universalistic to Particularistic Focus

After democratization, social movement organizations (those that strive for a collective public or categoric good) will often transform into interest associations (groups which are primarily concerned with providing selective benefits to their members). Combating an authoritarian regime requires that all activity be focused on the national level; personal development is often left unattended. After a transition to democracy, the organizations' goals or mission may change to a more inward focus. For example, Veronica Schild argues that (women's) organizations become spaces of learning, and begin to diverge from their original mission to focus on topics of sexuality, family life, literacy, and domestic abuse. She posits that although many organizations' original mission was related to human rights or poverty, many have now re-defined their mission to focus on personal growth and education (Schild, 1992: 9-13). Organizations may change their focus from purely political undertakings to include social, cultural, or sporting activities as well.

Political to Economic (or Social) Activity

During democratization, it is likely we will see a transition in those groups which relied upon international or non-governmental organization funding. This change will be from organizations which focus on highly political activities to those which place more emphasis on economic or entrepreneurial activity; this is necessitated by the withdrawal of funding from international and domestic donors. In order to survive, organizations must attain a minimal level of economic self-sufficiency. This focal change is also likely to occur in those countries which have recently undergone or are undergoing a process of economic liberalization; the mission or functions of a group may change to reflect the high profile given to neo-liberalism. In doing so, the organization would merely be adapting to its environment.

Goal-Oriented to Domain-Oriented

It is also important to look at an organization's goal(s). Under authoritarianism, some groups limit their activities and focus to one goal, such as the undermining of the regime. Yet "tunnel vision" on a specific goal will likely result in organizational disbanding when that goal is attained. Survival is more probable when an organization's goal is to function within a domain, not on a given mission. As discussed by Thompson, a goal is "some imagined state of affairs which may conceivably be attained or approached at some future time...The notion of domain is timeless" (Thompson, 1967: 127). For example, it would be easier for an organization to continue functioning if its focus were human rights in general, instead of limiting its scope to torture and disappearances by the military dictatorship. After the transition, such groups could transform to focus on rights and demands of women or children. This move from goal-oriented to domain-oriented groups parallels the transformation in organizations from social movements to interest associations, as discussed above.

Therefore, *after a transition to democracy, most organizations will spend more time on economic survival, mission re-definition, and social or cultural activities. The transformed organizations will be overwhelmingly self-focused and local.* Of course, since these are generalizations across a wide range of organizations, there will be exceptions within the path of organizational transformation, and there will be other paths as well. There are two types of organizations which are least likely to transform and adapt to the new environment. First, very recently-founded organizations will likely de-mobilize or be incorporated into political parties or the state; they will not have enough members, leaders, nor resources built up to out-live the temporary *bajón*. Second, groups whose singular goal is the end of the specific political system (such as the defeat of authoritarian rule) may also de-mobilize; if they are unable or unwilling to adopt a new set of goals, they will disband after the attainment of their original mission.

I began this project with the hypothesis that the organizations which would transform most successfully are those whose members are connected not only through an issue or goal, but are also motivated by similarities among members or a common identity. Such groups should also have an advantage because they can use their identity as an additional resource to win provisions and to mobilize members[39]. Therefore, I hypothesized that women's and ethnic groups would likely adapt better to the transition than other organizations.[40] As demonstrated in Chapter 6, my research proved this hypothesis to be incorrect; in that chapter I also explore the implications of a demobilized women's sector on democracy and its citizens.

Organizations make up civil society. So, if most organizations indeed follow a path of transformation, what will civil society look like after a transition to democracy? Under this framework, one can imagine that civil society will be both dynamic and diffuse. In the past, most theorists have described only a snapshot of civil society — a static description of a given moment. That is why democratization theorists have failed to capture the transformation of organizations — they isolate their study of civil society to the time prior to, or during, the transition. Snapshots do not capture a dynamic process; to see motion, we must view the pictures sequentially.[41] As Gerardo Munck claims, "Social movements must keep moving, expanding their identities, developing broader coalitions, taking on new issues, transforming their discourse" (Munck, 1991: 8). The organizations of civil society will continually adapt to meet the changing needs of the citizenry and to address the varying issues in politics. Organizations, like political systems, can transition to new forms or revert back to old forms. Networks with other organizations will be built and disbanded, alliances with parties will be established and ended, international funding will come and go. In response, most organizations will transform instead of de-mobilize. Civil society under democracy is a dynamic phenomenon.

The path of transformation also yields a diffuse civil society in which national hierarchical networks are fragmented but organizations become highly effective on the local level.[42] The emphasis is on horizontal, not vertical, relations between organizations. Organizations will relate more to the municipality and other local or neighborhood groups than to a social movement or national cause. The degree to which this is true may vary over time; however, it is only when there is a common, unifying enemy that organizations will converge again at a national level, as they did under authoritarianism.

In the rest of this book, I explore the theoretical conundrum about the effect of democratization upon civil society. In doing so, I will answer many of the questions posed above, and will undoubtedly leave others unanswered. My findings demonstrate that the story is more complex than any of the theorists had indicated; in fact, it seems that the reality is distinct from that which they have proposed as well as that which I had hypothesized before commencing my research. First, while overt "political"[43] participation is reduced significantly, citizens do continue to participate actively in the social, economic and cultural realms following a transition to democracy. Notwithstanding, most political organizations and their membership remain structurally and hierarchically intact, largely inactive except in response to crisis situations. There is therefore an organizational residue in the political realm. Second, groups with a common goal and a common identity may seem most likely to survive, but instead they may be among the weakest and may conform to the demobilization hypothesis. In the Chilean example, while many women have left the household, women's groups have failed to occupy the public space; feminist organizations may have been successful in getting women to participate, but their participation has been largely outside the traditionally political realm.

These findings have powerful implications for the stability, type and quality of democracy. In order to examine this argument, I combine democratization literature and organization theory with field research in Chile. My findings imply that those who study civil society by concentrating on the regime level and on national social movements miss a sizable portion of the action; with decentralization a growing reality, scholars must also look to the local level in order to understand participation after democratization.

CHILE: A KEYHOLE TO LOOKING AT CIVIL SOCIETY

This study examines how organizations respond to changes in their environment. In it, I focus primarily on the impact of a transition to democracy on civil society, and then I briefly outline the subsequent influence civil society may have on the consolidation of the regime. Civil society is, therefore, studied first as a dependent variable in the transition, and then as an independent variable in the consolidation of democracy. The focus of this book is on the trajectories of organizations that emerged and flourished under authoritarian rule.

Because an in-depth study of one organization alone would not indicate the density of civil society, this study should ideally have looked at the entire spectrum of organizations. Yet civil society is too vast a concept to cover in its entirety. Therefore, I chose to do a sampling of the range of possible organizational activity within civil society. In order to do so, I established that nearly every organization could be grouped under one of four categorizations: territorial, functional, identity and ideological. Of course, these categorizations are not mutually exclusive nor rigid; there are several groups that could fall into more than one category, or have changed categories over the course of their development. This organizational breakdown proved to be a useful heuristic tool in order to make civil society manageable as a variable; I limited my research to one or two types of organizations that are representative of each category.

"Territorial organizations" are those groups which form, function, and attract members primarily on the basis of locality."⁴⁴ In this project, the neighborhood associations (*Juntas de Vecinos*) and mothers' centers (*Centros de Madres*) are representative of territorial organizations. "Functional organizations" are groups that organize around a common goal, function or interest; they are usually utilitarian in nature. Here I focus on labor unions and popular economic organizations (sustenance groups). Those groups that coalesce principally because of the members' common self-identity, such as womanhood or ethnicity, are categorized as "identity organizations;" women's feminist groups will represent this category. Finally, "ideological organizations" are those whose primary impetus is the projection and attainment of a set of ideas, political or spiritual beliefs, or a shared doctrine. Political parties are the obvious choice here.

The specific organizations within each category were chosen to encompass a wide range of socio-economic levels, political tendencies, and both sexes. The challenge has been to research and write this book without discussing citizens and participants as if they were men. This is rendered somewhat difficult because women and women's groups are often segregated from the whole of civil society in academic studies. As a feminist scholar, one of my goals has been to give a voice to the diversity of women's experiences with political organizing — both as part of a women's movement and as part of the greater civil society. Research methods for this project included over one hundred interviews with organization leaders and members, interviews with government leaders, extended observation of the meetings and activities of two organizations in each of the above four categories, and archival reading. Research was conducted with the goal of mapping what trajectories organizations take after a transition to democracy, and identifying how civil society might impact the consolidation of democracy.

For two reasons, the organizations included in this study were limited to those whose base is in a major urban area. First, there is considerable difficulty in recording and attaining accurate information on organizations in rural areas, especially during an authoritarian regime. Second, with the exception of peasant movements, civil society is largely an urban phenomenon in late twentieth century Latin America; this is partially due to the financial and distance constraints encountered by those living in rural areas.[45]

Chile, both theoretically and empirically, provides an ideal keyhole through which to study the effect of democratization on civil society. In the Chilean case, one can separate to some extent, political from economic variables since the economic and political liberalizations did not occur simultaneously as they did in Eastern Europe. When both parts of society are liberalized at the same time, it is difficult to isolate the effect of each individually. Economic liberalization leads to an increased sense of competition and individualism among citizens, as well as a change in personal incomes and organizations' funding, which may have an effect upon participation patterns. However, this project proposed to study how a change in political environment effects organizations. Therefore, it was imperative to select a case in which I could isolate the effect of the independent variable, a transition to democracy, on civil society; Chile offers just such an opportunity.

Second, it was important to choose a country in which there existed more than just a semblance of participation; in Chile, civil society has long been one of the defining features of the political system. In the final decade of authoritarian rule, there was a proliferation of organizations; they are credited with pushing open political space in which to challenge Pinochet, attracting international attention to the human rights abuses in the country, and supplementing many households' declining food and income levels. There is thus much interest over whether these groups will continue to meet the needs and express the demands of the citizens.

Finally, Chile has undergone a recent process of re-democratization, which lends itself to innumerable questions about organizational memory and diffusion. Will groups revert to old patterns of organizing, or will they learn from past experiences or other countries' experiences and adopt new forms of organizing? The prior democratic regime was participatory, but heavily weighted toward political parties. With such a strong history of party dominance, if organizations maintain their autonomy from political parties and the state, they are likely to do so as well in the many other countries where parties have traditionally been less powerful. If, in

Chile, parties are no longer dominant, it would mean that there has not only been a significant transformation of the political system, but also of civil society. The existence of a strong party system will also facilitate a study of the relationships between civil and political society; do parties nurture or hinder citizens' participation?

CHAPTER OVERVIEW

Focusing on the peculiarities of the Chilean case within the Latin American region, Chapter 2 sketches the history of citizens' participation under the prior democratic regime, during authoritarian rule and through the initial phases of the transition to democracy. Within this context, I highlight the histories of the organizations that will serve as the case studies for this book. Chapters 3 through 6 apply my theoretical approach to the empirical field research on participation in Chile. Chapter 3 looks at the phenomena of mobilization versus de-mobilization. Although some organizations do experience a lessening in participation or activity, the "de-mobilization" or "de-politicization" is far from that predicted by O'Donnell and Schmitter. The majority of organizations continue to mobilize actively after democratization; yet the types and modes of participation have changed. Chapter 4 addresses the issue of the de-politicization and subsequent "economization" of participation. After a transition to democracy, the organizations of civil society become much less political and decidedly more economic in nature and action. As individuals become disillusioned with democracy, and groups are increasingly unable to compete with parties, civil society distances itself from the political realm. As international funding disappears and the neo-liberal model takes hold, groups often begin to sell products or services so that they can survive. While civil society re-organizes itself in less overtly political realms, it also re-groups and focuses on the local arena. The localization of civil society is the focus of Chapter 5. Paralleling the national trend toward decentralization, organizations are flourishing on the local level, yet almost defunct in the national arena. There has also been a simultaneous transformation in the foci of many organizations. Groups have changed from being other-focused to self-focused, from having universalistic goals to particularistic plans. Chapter 6

tracks and analyzes the unique case of women's participation in
Chile. The high levels of women's organizing and leadership in the
political opposition during the 1980s led many to be optimistic
about their future role under democracy. Yet at the present
moment, women are weakly represented in leadership positions in
the government, political parties and citizens' organizations.
Furthermore, a substantial number of feminist groups have disbanded since the transition to civilian rule. Such a phenomenon is
counter to my original hypothesis about the survivability of identity groups; what went awry with women's organizing?

The empirical chapters thus paint a picture of a post-transition
civil society which is active and largely local, particularistic and
economic in nature, with the notable and crucial exception of feminist organizing. The concluding chapter analyzes what this new
configuration of civil society means for issues of representation and
citizenship, and how it might affect the quality, type and stability of
democracy whether it be in Chile or in one of the many other societies in transition.

Notes

1.   Bertita Benavente, former vice-president of the women's
Voluntariado, interview with the author on August 17, 1994.

2.   Winnie Lira, director of the *Fundación Solidaridad*, interview with the
author on August 3, 1994.

3.   Civil society is the collectivity of self-constituted organizations outside of the family unit or firm and the state, which expresses or meets the
needs or interests of groups of citizens. Note that in this study, civil society will be examined apart from "political society," which is the arena
wherein actors (such as political parties) competitively vie for control of
the State (Diamond, 1992: 7). Herein, the organizations of civil society are
also referred to as "citizens' organizations."

4.   For de Toqueville's argument on associations under democracy, see
his *Democracy in America*, Book 1, Part 1, and Book 2.

5. For an excellent discussion of civil society in advanced industrialized countries, see Schmitter (1993), Schmitter and Streck (1985), and Bendix (1990). Among the best studies of civil society in developing countries are those of Jaquette (1989), Alvarez (1990), Oxhorn (1995), León (1994), and Schneider (1995).

6. Democratization" is the process of arriving at a consolidated democracy; it is also referred to as the process of a "transition to democracy". This period is characterized by a large degree of uncertainty about the rules, norms and about the future outcome of the political system; it is also the time in which the opposition begins to believe that there is a new means to effect change (see O'Donnell and Schmitter, 1986).

7. There is some evidence that the democratic wave may now be hitting parts of Africa. Huntington (1991) argues that this is only the third wave of democratization. He argues that the first wave lasts from 1826 until 1926, which encompasses Karl and Schmitter's first and second waves.

8. Colitt, Raymond. 1997. "Latin America Reforms 'Fail to Cut Income Disparities': Despite a Big Increase in Inequality, the Multilateral Lending Institutions Warn of Back-tracking." *Financial Times*. November 13. p. 7.

9. Burges, Sean W. 1998. "Don't Ignore the Dark Side." *Journal of Commerce*. April 16. p. 6A.

10. This is akin to de Toqueville's argument about the French Revolution that "steadily increasing prosperity, far from tranquilizing the population, everywhere promoted a spirit of unrest." As quoted in Huntington, 1968, p. 50.

11. This is known as Huntington's "democratic distemper" argument.

12. As discussed and cited in Pateman, 1970: 7–10.

13. See Canel's argument about Uruguay in Escobar and Alvarez, 1992, Chapter 15.

14. Such support comes in many different forms — funding, materials, networks, advice.

15. A pacted transition is a transition which occurs largely due to "explicit (though not always public) agreements between contending actors, which define the rules of governance on the basis of mutual guarantees for the 'vital interests' of those involved" (Karl, 1990: 9).

16. Canel's example is the case of Uruguay, which underwent a process of re-democratization during which social movements emerged late in the transition period and, he argues, declined rapidly.

17. Schmitter (1993: 8–11) addresses most of these factors.

18. While Rousseau values participation, he looks down upon representation; in *On Social Contract* he argues, "the moment a people allows itself to be represented, it is no longer free." Therefore, town meetings, self-help organizations, and public forums are considered acceptable, whereas as implicitly, political parties are not because they are the embodiment of representation. For a more in-depth discussion of Rousseau's conceptions of participation versus representation, see Benjamin Barber's "Political Participation and the Creation of Res Publica" in Ritter (1988), pp. 292–306.

19. The causality in this argument can be questioned. Participation may indeed lead citizens to have a "stake" in the political system; but this relationship may also be reversed. Citizens may choose to participate precisely because they have a "stake" in the system.

20. For an excellent discussion of participatory democracy and its theorists, see Pateman (1970).

21. With the exception of the literature on voting abstention, the issue of individuals' participation has largely been left out of this debate about the desirability and stability of participation in democracy.

22. The term "democratization literature" denotes the scholarly work on transitions to and from democratic rule.

23. Those familiar with the work of Richard Scott will note that my perspective of an organization is concurrent with Scott's definition of an Open System, in which "Organizations are systems of interdependent activities linking shifting coalitions of participants; the systems are embedded in — dependent on continuing exchanges with and constituted by — the environments in which they operate" (Scott, 1992: 25).

24. In fact, some argue that merging is the same as disappearing; when the "structure of the organization changes radically as it merges, so that it no longer manifests the form in evidence before the merger, this is counted as an ending" (Hannan and Freeman, 1989: 151).

25. The Townsend Movement formed in the United States in the 1930s, around the issue of national pensions for the elderly. When the Depression ended, the organization had to end or transform because other

older-aged groups sprung up and created competition. First the Townsend Movement transformed to focus on state instead of national legislation. It then went from selling goal-oriented auto-stickers and buttons, and began selling soap, vitamins, and candy. Finally, the focus and draw of Townsend Movement meetings became card-playing and recreation instead of pensions (See Messinger, 1955: 5–10).

26. For Denton and Zald, organizational "success" is defined as an organization that is not demobilizing, is flexible, and is always enlarging its membership. While I would agree with their first two measures (not demobilizing and flexible), I find fault with their last one. Organizations without an "always enlarging membership" may still be seen as successful; their membership level may have found a balance (i.e., it is constant), or the organization may have chosen to enhance its stability, efficiency or activism by *choosing* to decrease or hold constant its membership.

27. Zald and Denton also include the following in their reasons of why the YMCA has been successful: Not dominated by a single religion. Driven by fees and necessity to enroll members — an enrollment economy. Low level of professional ideology. Adaptive to community needs.

28. I should begin by noting that the best effort put forth thus far in answering this question is by Philippe Schmitter (1993); however, his analysis still depicts civil society as a static and inflexible entity.

29. Methodologically, path choice may be seen as the dependent variable of this framework.

30. See Mainwaring (1987) and Jacquette (1994) for more on cooptation of social movements and organizations following a transition to democracy.

31. Whereas democratization is the independent variable, these factors may be seen as the intervening variables of the project; the ensuing empirical chapters explore the causal links between these factors and the dependent variable (path choice).

32. Likewise, a loss of political autonomy may occur when fifty percent or more of an organization's political agenda or objectives is dictated by another entity.

33. A dramatic decrease in funding might also serve as evidence of a group's impending de-mobilization.

34. For an extensive description of the characteristics of transitions, particularly that of uncertainty, see O'Donnell and Schmitter, 1986.

35.   This argument is that of James Thompson (1967).

36.   See Philippe Schmitter (1986, 1993).

37.   Tarrow writes, "but as the flood tide recedes, there are more concrete sediments as well (Zolberg, 1972). New levies of political participants gain their initial socialization during such periods. The archetypal themes of collective action employed then are handed down to the future which with the scent of the collective enthusiasm in which they were born. New SMOs are formed and imprint the issues around which they were born in their future programs and ideologies. Most important, except where an authoritarian inversion follows, the forms of collective action invented at the peak of the cycle are extended and quasi-institutionalized into its declining phase stretching the boundaries of the conventional repertoire even as the society goes back to a phase of de-mobilization." His argument focuses on how the structure of political opportunity effects social movements; herein, I suggest that the political opportunity structure is just one piece of the puzzle.

38.   For example, municipalization is occurring (or has occurred) in Chile, Argentina, Peru, and Colombia where laws or constitutions have been changed to give more power to local governments. It is still unclear whether El Salvador, Guatemala, or Haiti will follow a similar path. See Borja (1989 and 1987).

39.   This idea was first introduced to me through conversations with Dominque Blom. See her related argument in Blom, 1992.

40.   For this hypothesis, I am indebted to Elena Vergen, a community development worker in the Chilean municipality of Lo Espejo (interview 1992) whose insightful comments sparked my thinking in this area.

41.   This reminds me of de Toqueville's (1762/9156) argument on a related subject about the necessity of looking at the lifetime of an object of interest: "If a certain moment in the existence of a nation be selected, it is easy to prove that political associations perturb the state and paralyze productive industry; but take the whole life of a people, and it may perhaps be easy to demonstrate, that freedom of association in political matters is favorable to the prosperity, and even to the tranquillity, of the community."

42.   The reader may wish to contrast this concept of "diffusion" with March's notion of "organized anarchies" in which organizations have fluid participation, ill-defined preferences, and unclear technology and processes (March, 1988: 294–6).

43.   Scholars and practitioners will — and should — have a problem with this narrow approach to defining the "political." As a feminist, I too

cringe at the suggestion that the "political" realm can be cordoned off from the personal or socio-cultural realm. Yet for the purposes — and more importantly, in the findings — of this study, "political" actions herein denote when organizations seek to participate in or affect the system, institutions, policies or actors of government. With this understanding, I will no longer use quotation marks to flag the limitations of using the word political in such a context. See Chapter 4 for a more complete discussion of the meanings of political.

44.   In Chile, territorial organizations are defined within the law. Diario Oficial Law #18.893 (December 30, 1989) defines territorial organizations as those "whose goal is the development of the *comuna* and the interests of its inhabitants in the respective territory and who cooperate with the authorities of the State in the Municipalities."

45.   For an overview of the challenges of rural areas, see J. Fox (ed.), *The Challenge of Rural Democratization: Perspectives from Latin America and the Philippines,"* London: Frank Cass, 1990.

CHAPTER TWO

Organizing the Past:

Participation and Civil Society in Chile

> We may be little, but we think
> participation plays a very important
> role in democracy. If the government
> does not have connection to the base
> (masses), it would be a unilateral
> government. A weak government. It
> would soon be an extinct government.[1]

When investigating contemporary political topics, an historical overview can at times appear to be a digression or a distraction from the question at hand; however, with the topic at hand, history can provide us with the tools to understand how emerging democracies affect organized participation. There are four ways in which history proves useful. First, looking at history provides clues for studying contemporary phenomena. Knowing how and where organizations acted and interacted under a prior democracy yields a preliminary road map for scholars to use to locate and to understand citizens' participation after re-democratization. Second, an historical survey allows us to recognize if and how a change in environment produces subsequent and parallel changes in the sub-environment. For example, an overview of civil society prior to Chile's 1973 military coup is essential if this research is to identify if and how organizational structures and relationships under the emerging democracy differ from those under the previous democratic regime. This is also true for the potential dissimilarities in civil society under military versus democratic rule. Third, most academic works on civil society focus on one particular type of organization; such a focus yields a study rich in depth and detail, but fails to provide an accurate portrait of the whole of organized participation. Therefore, a general overview of the history of citizens' organizations will allow for a study of the variations of, as well as within, civil society over time. Finally, political science, in addition to explaining current phenomena, should also be able to reinterpret past phenomena; it should be able to re-illuminate aspects of history by asking questions in a way that would not have been done in the past. Current advances in democratization theory and organization theory may shed new light on the interplay between participation and democracy under the prior regime in Chile. The organizations elaborated in this chapter are those which serve as case studies in the ensuing chapters. The history and details of feminist organizing I have left for Chapter 6, since I offer a contrasting argument about the trajectory of those groups. This chapter does not intend to be a comprehensive study of all of civil society organizing; instead, it calls attention to the high and low points of organizing, as well as mobilization patterns. While this chapter details the specific historical context of Chile, I have found many of the general comments provided herein to be useful when studying transitions to democracy in other Latin American countries.

PARTICIPATION UNDER DEMOCRACY: 1930s–1973

Up to this point, I have referred to "transitions to democracy" and "democratization." However many of the Latin American cases are actually examples of a transition *back* to democracy or *re*-democratization. The 1960s and early 1970s saw a wave of authoritarianism engulf Latin America, collapsing seven of the democracies in South America alone, including in the southern cone countries of Argentina, Uruguay and Chile. It is important to locate the Chilean case in the context of a return to democratic rule in a country historically known for its deep and wide-reaching party system, a strong and penetrating Catholic Church, and few traditions of state corporatism.

Until its military coup in 1973, Chile claimed the longest running democracy in Latin America with a strong justice system, fair elections, civilian rule over the military, and active political parties.[2] Organized, and highly politicized, participation also flourished in Chile under the prior democratic regime. Although somewhat sporadic, unions continually grew in number and power; by 1970, 30 percent of the labor market was affiliated with a union. Neighborhood organizations (*Juntas de Vecinos*), peasant associations and the mothers' centers (*Centros de Madres*, CEMAs) also demonstrated similar growth patterns in the 1960s. Some scholars suggest that by 1973, there were approximately one million *pobladores* participating in citizens' organizations; a number which does not even include the mothers' centers. This is an astounding level of participation considering that in 1973, the Chilean population numbered around 10.5 million.[3]

The development of Chilean civil society under the prior democracy was erratic, with periods of stagnation interspersed with spurts of great momentum. In large part, the participation "booms" coincided with four state policies: import substituting industrialization (ISI), extending the right of suffrage to women, Frei's citizens' participation initiative, and Allende's socialist experiment. The intervals between participation booms were marked by high levels of inactivity within civil society, during which political parties were among the few groups to remain mobilized.[4] In fact, the parties were the loci of participation under the prior democratic regime, and tended either to outlast or co-opt other types of organizations.[5]

Import substituting industrialization helped give rise to the first major participation boom in the prior democratic period. In response to a perceived negative terms of trade and a decreasing availability of products due to World War II, the Chilean government, like many other Latin American governments, began an ISI development program. Designed with the goal of producing domestically those products which were previously imported, one of ISI's side-effects was an increased mobilization of some social sectors. By promoting the industrialization of the country, ISI opened the way for stronger industrial unions and the unionization of state employees, as the power and numbers of the industrial sector grew. Fifty-four percent of small firms, 60 percent of medium

firms, and 35 percent of large firms existing in Chile in 1970 were
founded under ISI between 1931-1950 (Petras, 1970: 43).

Labor affiliation soared as a reflection of industrialization;
between 1936 and 1946 the number of union workers increased by
190% (Frías, 1993: 12). The new affiliates in Chile belonged largely
to the socialist-communist *Central de Trabajadores de Chile* (CTCH)
which was founded in 1936 and had its base among industrial, min-
ing, construction and service workers. The CTCH dominated labor
organizing in Chile until 1946, when it divided into two separate
organizations: some of the unions were absorbed by the coalition
of middle-class-led organizations called the Popular Front (*Frente
Popular*), and the rest became part of the leftist Central Federation
of Workers (*Central Unica de Trabajadores*, CUT) which formed in 1953;
the latter was to occupy the most visible and most powerful position in Chilean labor organizing for the next several decades.
Public employees also gained power with the founding of the
Asociación Nacional de Empleados Fiscales (ANEF) in 1943. The Chilean
labor sector became among the strongest and most organized in
Latin America.

Yet even though unions gained more (although still limited)
freedom to organize during the industrialization phase, they
remained notably subjugated to the Chilean state and political parties; the Popular Front coalition, the Chilean Socialist Party and the
Radical Party claimed the greatest control over unions, serving as
their channels of representation. The labor movement, although
growing in number and strength, flourished largely as a reflection
of the political parties — a pattern which was to persist until the
military coup of 1973. This pattern was established not only
because of the uncontestable strength of the parties, but also
because of the limited channels of interest representation available
to civil society as well as the legal restrictions placed upon union
organizing. Since the return to democratic rule, most of these
obstacles to union autonomy have disappeared or decreased.[6]

The second burst in citizens' participation came with the
debate over women's suffrage, which I have detailed in Chapter 6.
The decades of the 1930s and 1940s in Chile were marked by a proliferation of women's organizations demanding the right to vote.

Although they would not have self-identified as such due to societal stigmatisms, these suffrage groups were part of a widespread
middle- and upper-class feminist movement in which they questioned the way women were inserted into the electoral and political structure of the country. In contrast to labor organizations,
these feminist groups enjoyed absolute autonomy from the political parties. The suffrage movement remained an isolated, but powerful sector of civil society; it was, in fact, the only citizens' sector
prior to 1973 which gained significant autonomy from the parties.

The third participation boom, instigated by *Promoción Popular*,
centered most of its impulse on the territorial organizations of civil
society. *Promoción Popular* was a government program created by
Christian Democratic President Eduardo Frei in 1964 to provide the
financial and material resources necessary to start or convert community organizations into self-help groups so that they could
address and resolve neighborhood problems. This program was
largely established through the neighborhood associations and
mothers' centers, with much involvement by the local government.
The neighborhood councils were encouraged to focus on issues of
water, sanitation, and education in the communities.[7] The three
functions of the mothers' centers were: teaching skills women
might use to supplement their household income, giving child-
rearing classes, and holding social events. Both of these organizations had previously been associated with or aided by the Catholic
Church. The available resources combined with the guaranteed
channel of interest representation through *Promoción Popular*
increased the energy and organizational incentives of civil society.
Between 15,000 and 20,000 organizations were involved with
Promoción Popular (Petras, 1970: 231), over 8,000 of which were
CEMAs, involving some 400,000 women (Silva Donoso, 1987: 57).
Promoción Popular exemplified the state corporatist ideology of the
Chilean government prior to 1973; the approach was to encourage
community organizing as a form of development, but to keep it regulated. However, in contrast to the prior two participation swells,
this time the institutionalization occurred more through the state,
and not the political parties.[8]

The final burst of participation happened during the years
(1970-1973) of President Salvador Allende's Popular Unity (*Unidad*

Popular, UP) government and its experiment with socialism. During the years of Allende, union organizing increased dramatically. Affiliation rose from an all-time Chilean high of 27.4% in 1971, to a 1973 record of 32.3% (Frías, 1993: 15). The CUT continued to dominate labor organizing during this period, increasing its number of affiliated unions and federations to 130 in 1973; this was up from 87 in 1970. This increase in labor organizing was partially a reflection of the favored and therefore facilitated role of the worker in Allende's socialist experiment, and partially a function of the dramatic economic problems those same workers were confronting. Between October 1972 and March 1973, the cost of living in Chile increased by 76.2%. Of three thousand basic products, over five hundred were unavailable in the stores and citizens waited in line for hours for their food rations. Prices on the black market skyrocketed beyond the reach of the lower and middle classes (Whelan, 1989: 403, 315).

In December of 1971, thousands of women — perhaps the largest women's demonstration in Chile up to that point — took to the streets to protest the food shortages and long lines. Union strikes gained momentum. It was, in fact, these women's marches together with the unions which first led the opposition's uprising against Allende.[9] Through extensive strikes, the copper and trucking unionists protested the lowering of wages, inflation, and the nationalization program. Beginning in April of 1973, the 11,500 workers at El Teniente copper mine went on strike for nearly three months to demand wage increases. Teachers and students joined the copper miners. By the time the strike ended, it had cost Chile almost US$60 million in copper revenues. Again that year, in July, the trucking unions went on strike; with their 160,000 bodies and 75,000 trucks they virtually immobilized the Chilean transportation system when 110,000 bus and taxi drivers joined forces with them (Whelan, 1989: 403, 409). These unionists dealt particularly strong blows to the economy and eventually to the political legitimacy of Allende by paralyzing trade and transportation within the country. Yet despite the increased numbers and activities of unions, the labor movement remained divided and somewhat institutionalized by political parties (particularly by the socialist and communist parties) throughout Allende's rule. With the exception of the marches under Allende, the women's movement remained notably absent during the early 1970s, while the neighborhood councils and mothers' centers displayed only moderate participation, reminiscent of the years preceding Frei. No sector of civil society could challenge the frenzied activity of the unions under Allende.

However active, civil society was considerably fragmented during these participation "booms." There were many organized sectors, yet little communication and resource-sharing existed between organizations within the same domain, and far less between associations of different spheres. Church groups kept their distance from cultural organizations; neighborhood associations rarely teamed up with women's groups. Organizations cultivated few horizontal ties. For example, between 1938 and 1973 the unions were able to influence directly the governing of the state through negotiations, and indirectly through their influence with political parties; but they rarely worked in conjunction with other organizations to influence policy. Such was the case with most citizens' organizations; their most important and visible links remained with the state or political parties.

It was the political parties which unified the fragmentary interests of civil society (Mainwaring, 1987: 147); in fact, political parties or the state reigned over most organizations in Chile until the military coup. This pattern was initiated in 1949, after the women's vote was won and political parties began to incorporate (or some might argue, co-opt) the women's organizations by adopting some of their policy recommendations and encouraging women to declare party affiliations.[10] Parties were quick to woo the women, recognizing a large and untapped voter base. By the late 1950s few of the original women's groups were still in existence, having lost out to the political parties, and to organizational inertia.

From the mid-20th century until 1973, political parties continued to be the predominant force in civil society, with a three-way power balance between the Left, the Center, and the Right. Chile was a model of the Huntingtonian society, in which institutionalization both preceded and prevailed over participation; political parties played a leading role in this equation. In fact, under the prior democratic regime, there were just two occasions in which the power of citizens' organizations rivaled that of the parties. The first is that of the aforementioned women's organizations during the height of their suffrage campaign in the years leading up to 1949. To a lesser extent, the labor unions in the years under Allende can be considered as the second example.

Some, perhaps correctly, have argued that the strength of Chilean political parties created an obstacle to the development of civil society, which then played a significant role in the breakdown of democracy (Oxhorn, 1992: chapter 2).[11] Prior to 1973, parties were the pivotal point in the political sphere, and also in the social and economic realms (Garretón, 1986: 165). It was both easy and natural for organizations to become dependent upon the parties for supplementary funds, resources or contacts. In this manner, citizens' groups grew weak and unable to express or meet their demands autonomously; instead, organizations channeled their demands and requested funds through the parties. Civil society looked to the parties for assistance, and the government turned to the parties for support or policy input.[12] In the early 1970s, there were few opportunities for citizens to present their demands directly to the government; with the exception of the unions, parties became the only method for channeling and representing demands and needs. Civil society, in effect, became isolated and stagnant in the face of the dominant parties. Yet with the advent of authoritarian rule, political parties were the first to lose their place at center stage; and with democratization, they were to be one of the last to regain it.

The perpetrators of the Chilean military coup of September 11, 1973 sought to end the wave of polarization which had swept over the country between left and right, between traditional and progressive, and between socialist and capitalist. Towards this end, they tried to de-activate the parties and organizations and the linkages between them, and to stop all forms of political participation. The ideal state which they envisioned was one free from pressure from below, with very little input in the decision-making processes. Like Huntington (1968), the military leaders regarded societal order and citizens' participation as incompatible; therefore, it was the latter which would have to go.

CIVIL SOCIETY UNDER AUTHORITARIAN RULE: 1973–1990

Authoritarianism and civil society are often viewed to be in an adversarial relationship; the existence of either one may endanger the other. Authoritarian rulers will likely suppress opposition organizations (or at times, all organizations); and civil society, if allowed to mobilize, may de-legitimize a dictatorial regime.[13] It is important to understand the role of civil society under authoritarianism if we are to establish how it changes with a transition to democracy.[14]

In order to retain power over a country, dictatorial rulers need to control the dissemination of information, dissenting opinions, and any activities which might de-legitimize their regime. For that reason, a transition to authoritarian rule often begins with a dismantling of political and civil society. Political parties, non-governmental organizations, neighborhood associations, and independent media which do not support the new government are shut down. Large group meetings, rallies, and public opinion polls may be disallowed. Such rules may be explicitly spelled out in governmental law or decree as they were in the "harder" authoritarian regimes like Chile or El Salvador, or they may be more like common law "understandings" imposed by a "softer" regime, as in Mexico. And in all too many cases, those who challenge the new rules, particularly organization leaders, find themselves victims of human rights abuses — torture, disappearances, or executions.[15] Fear pervades much of the populace. With its realms of activity severely limited and the lives of its members possibly endangered, civil society becomes immobilized; it can neither retain its prior organizations, nor start up new associations. Out of fear for the lives and well-being of themselves and their families, citizens may hesitate or refuse to participate in organizations. Many sectors of civil society are thus exiled from the political system, while others remain in a state of self-imposed exile.

It is important to note that organizations are not non-existent under authoritarian rule; in Chile, as in Argentina, El Salvador, Uruguay and many other Latin American countries, some groups remain active during this period. Under authoritarianism, there are actually two realms of organizing: the official (government-con-doned) and the clandestine (government-repressed) realms. In Chile, mostly business associations, pro-military and conservative pro-democracy groups comprised the former; the latter were large-ly human rights, church-based, labor, and opposition organiza-tions. In Chile, the *diario oficial* law #349 (March 13, 1974) gave the government the right to ask for the resignation of organization leaders at any time and to appoint a replacement. This was appli-cable to all neighborhood associations, mothers' centers, and other community and functional organizations. Also by govern-ment decree, all such groups were reviewed and those that were seen as leftist or against the regime were stripped of their legal sta-tus (*personalidad jurídica*). Three years later, the municipalities, whose leaders were appointed by the military regime, were encour-aged by the Ministry of the Interior to dissolve or control such organizations. Such repressive measures severely curtailed the activity of the neighborhood associations, relegating them to be mostly ceremonial entities.

The military government also sought to harness labor union organizing. During the first six years of the dictatorship, collective negotiation was disallowed, as were strikes and protest marches. Such laws disrupt the fundamentals of union activity and severely hamper their existence; from the viewpoint of labor, union-man-agement disputes are nearly impossible to win when the tradition-al tools and strategies of labor are outlawed. It was not until 1979 that the laws against collective negotiation were revoked—but it was after the power of the unions had been largely dismantled and under conditions that continued to be detrimental to union organ-izing: high levels of unemployment (18% and growing), the right to replace striking workers after 30 days, and government regulation of collective negotiation (Campero and Cortazar, 1988).

Not only did union activity come to a near standstill in the 1970s in Chile, but there was very little organizing throughout civil society, particularly among opposition forces. CONAR (the Committee to Help Refugees) was one of the first such groups founded in September of 1973; its goal was to help those foreign-ers who had sought refuge in Chile from the dictatorship and repression in their home countries, and then found themselves in difficulty when Chile, too, became repressive. In October of the same year, COPACHI (the Committee of Cooperation for Peace in Chile) was formed to work for a non-violent end to authoritarian rule, but then dissolved in 1975 because of government pressure. COPACHI led to the founding of the *Vicaría de la Solidaridad*, a Catholic Church-based human rights organization which helped Chileans locate their families and friends who had disappeared, and which eventually took on a more general human rights, anti-military stance. Also in 1973, the Association of Democratic Women (*Agrupación de Mujeres Democráticas*) was started to support families repressed by the military government and to denounce human rights violations. In the labor realm, the only notable organizing that was done in the 1970s was by the National Labor Coordinator (*Coordinadora Nacional Sindical*, CNS) which formed in 1978 in order to re-gain broad workers' rights. With the exception of the aforementioned groups and the pro-military organizations, notable among which were the Society to Promote Manufacturing (*Sociedad para el Fomento de Fabricación*, SOFOFA) and the government-sponsored mothers' centers (CEMAs), there was little movement in civil society in Chile during the middle and late 1970s. Any organizing which might have been construed as against the military regime was met with severely repressive measures.[16]

Such a period of forced inactivity takes a heavy toll on organizations. Contacts and networks unravel. Resources become unavailable. Leadership skills decay. Avenues for teaching democratic values disappear. Generation(s) may grow up without learning how to participate or lead. Civil society begins to dissipate.

The subsequent process of re-birth is difficult for civil society; forming organizations, defining goals, finding funds and resources —almost all is done clandestinely.[17] Oxhorn argues that such a (re-)organization of civil society is a direct result of authoritarian rule; repression triggers the need and desire to organize.[18] This was certainly the case in Chile when small groups of citizens began mobilizing again around 1978. Activity then reaches even higher levels when the regime begins a process of liberalization. Such a process can be provoked by an economic crisis or boom, international pressure, or an internal conflict between hardliners and soft-

ation leads to an opening
of political space. Citizens expand their organizing, enter the political space and push it further open. This begins what O'Donnell
and Schmitter (1986) term the "resurrection or re-birth of civil society." In Chile, the economic boom of the late 1970s and very early
1980s led to an increase in the populace's confidence in the military government. As real salaries rose by 8 percent a year and
unemployment fell to 15%, the government, sensing a boost in citizen support, initiated a process of political liberalization — eliminating some of the restrictions on free speech, as well as on union
and community organizing.

Even in those countries with a history of strong political parties, such as in Chile, parties rarely take the predominant position
in these early stages of a transition. This is for two reasons. First,
political parties are often outlawed until the final stages of an
authoritarian regime. It is thus difficult for them to mobilize without severe and repressive consequences. Second, their *raison-d'être*
does not exist since authoritarianism functions outside of the electoral realm; without elections, parties would be relegated to the
same realm as other civil society organizations. Therefore, since
political parties are not an option, citizens have to find or create
other channels of participation; consequently, it is organizations
that play a dominant role in the resurrection of civil society
(O'Donnell and Schmitter, 1986). Even the right-leaning political
parties in Chile were "on recess" during the first years of the military regime, not resurfacing until the late 1970s.

Led by the human rights groups mentioned above and labor
unions, Chilean civil society began to re-emerge actively in the
early 1980s. On May 11, 1983 the first National Protest was called
by the Confederation of Copper Workers (CTC), followed by similar
protests in June, July and August of the same year. The Chilean
Armed Forces reacted with brutal force, imposed a dawn-to-dusk
curfew, and militarized the streets. These National Protests incorporated wide-ranging segments of the population: workers, women
and human rights activists denouncing the abuse of the dictatorship, and also those from the middle and upper-middle classes
objecting to the economic crisis. In the fourth protest, there were
twenty-eight deaths and over one hundred wounded. These

protests marked the beginning of a high level of anti-authoritarian mobilization which was dominated by the lower-income classes but also included the participation of some sectors of the upper-middle class. These mobilizations and the subsequent repressive measures taken by the government sparked the formation of the National Workers' Command (*Comando Nacional de Trabajadores*, CNT), the Movement of Women *Pobladoras* (*Movimiento de Mujeres Pobladoras*, MOMUPO), the resurrection of student unions, and the politicization of the Popular Economic Organizations (*organizaciones económicas populares*, OEPs).

Union organizing in the 1980s was dominated by two labor confederations: the National Workers' Command (CNT), and the Workers' Democratic Central (*Central Democrática de Trabajadores*, CDT), both of whom were very loosely connected to the Christian Democratic Party, with the CNT representing the more progressive side.[20] There were no strong labor unions linked to the state under military rule. Among opposition forces, it was far and away the CNT/CUT which represented more unions and could mobilize more citizens; in 1988, 73% of unionized workers in Chile attended the (re-)founding congress of the CUT (Frías, 1993: 47). Throughout the 1980s in Chile, unions had a strong presence at the national level, a leading role in the anti-authoritarian movement, much autonomy from political parties and the state, and a high degree of politicization. As stated by the president of the Copper and Petroleum Confederation, union organizing "has a political connotation, not a *política-partidista* (connotation),... but a political connotation because of the circumstances which Chile is living."[21] The military regime responded to the political and anti-authoritarian organizing of the unions with severe repression; nearly 150 unionists were disappeared, and thousands were detained, tortured or exiled.[22]

Unions led the anti-authoritarian push within civil society along with the Catholic Church-supported human rights groups and Popular Economic Organizations (*organizaciones económicas populares*, OEPs). "OEP" is the term used in Chile for those groups that began to arise in the early 1980s out of a need to supplement their household income or food levels, and in some cases to protest the dictatorship. Examples of OEPs are soup kitchens (*ollas comunes*), artisan workshops (*talleres productivos*), shopping cooperatives (*com-*

prando juntos), and communal planting groups (*huertos*). Their funding and support came largely from the Catholic Church's *Vicaría* and
from international donations. OEPs were, and still are, almost
exclusively comprised of women and are further discussed in
Chapter 6. These women were, in large part, on the political left or
center; although it was not politics, but concern for the economic
survival of their households which first prompted women to organize.[23] Authoritarianism not only prompted a proliferation of groups
which were largely comprised of women, but it also led to the
founding of innumerable feminist organizations promoting and
developing women's rights, education, and political access.

The organizations of a "resurrected" civil society therefore fulfill
numerous roles. They supplement food and income levels. They
teach skills. They serve as a means of voicing political concerns
through protest, artisan crafts, and strikes. Some use organizations
as a way to form a community based on a common identity, such as
gender or ethnicity. There may also arise organizations which channel funds from international donors to local groups, such as non-
governmental organizations. An active civil society can prove to be
an effective means to attract international attention to human
rights abuses, and to pressure authoritarian leaders for democratic
concessions; conversely, civil society can also support authoritarian rule.

The resurrection of civil society is often not just a steady climb
upward, but instead comes in waves. There often occur spurts of
mobilization followed by severe repression by the government, and
then a subsequent break in mobilization before the next wave. In
Chile, after the 1983 National Protests mobilized nearly one million
citizens against the dictatorship, there was a significant decline in
civil society activity in 1984 and 1985. This decrease in participation was due to two reasons. First, the high levels of repression
which follow a wave of mobilization instill much fear in the population and some people are likely to re-evaluate the costs of their
participation. Second, organizations (much like armies) often need
to step back, re-group, assess the impact they have made and
decide on their next course of action.[24] Despite the participatory
pull-back, much is learned during this initial burst of mobilization.
There occurs a process of confidence-building among activists

upon seeing the number of people behind the same cause. Organization leaders are able to establish new contacts and networks. Citizens learn about the government's reaction — how, where and to what extent they respond — so as to better plan the next round of mobilization. Organizations on the political right are also affected by these waves in mobilization under authoritarianism. In reaction to the mobilizations, conservative groups must increase their pro-government campaigning, defending the virtues of the military regime to both the domestic and international community. The activities of a resurrected civil society may, although not necessarily, have an impact on a transition to democracy.

PARTICIPATING IN A TRANSITION TO DEMOCRACY

A transition to democracy occurs when a country moves from non-democratic rule (i.e., totalitarianism or authoritarianism) toward some type of democratic regime. It is that interlude between two systems of governance — when the rules and outcome of the game are uncertain — that is known as the "transition."[25] It is the time in which the political environment and rules are changing, yet it is unclear what the end result will yield. In Chile, the transition began around 1987, just prior to the 1988 plebescite vote on whether to continue with the military regime (SI vote) or end it (NO vote). After years of clandestine preparation, organizations were poised to take advantage of this period of uncertainty, to convince citizens to vote against the dictatorship and to push elites to accept democracy. As center-stage in the anti-authoritarian crusade moved from the streets to the polls, political parties re-captured the limelight after a fifteen year absence.

After civil society begins its "resurrection," political parties then re-group when the possibility of electoral competition arises. In some cases, such as in Chile, this marks a significant change in participation patterns as questions of resource-sharing, autonomy and competition develop between organizations and parties. In Chile, political parties began to re-emerge gradually around 1983, although they did not truly gain any power or momentum until just prior to the 1988 plebescite when in April of 1987 the ban on public meetings by political parties was officially lifted. Party networking, and a semblance of party organizing, was already the norm in a semi-clandestine manner for years at that point. Parties of the right, beginning with the Democratic Independent Union (UDI), were the first to emerge publicly and mobilize in the late 1970s. However, with the ban lifted, the conservative parties merged to form a new party: the National Renewal Party (*Partido de Renovación Nacional*, RN).[26] The parties of the center and left entered public space more cautiously in the mid-1980s, led by the Christian Democratic Party (PDC), the Socialist Party (PS) and the Communist Party (PC). It is important to note that it is not the case that political parties ever completely disappeared during the late 1970s and early 1980s. In fact, often party leaders or ideology continued clandestinely to influence civil society organizing from the side-lines throughout the dictatorship.

In some cases, such as in Chile, the (re-)emergence of political parties may coincide with the transition; yet in other instances, like that of El Salvador, parties may appear well before the transition even begins. The existence of parties signals the presence of elections, however, elections most certainly do not indicate the existence of democracy nor even a transition to such a regime.[27] Notwithstanding, by the time a democratic transition is in full-swing, parties will have (re-)surfaced. During a transition, political parties are effective in two realms. First, by connecting with their counterparts in other countries, they are able to attract international attention to the abuses of the authoritarian regime. Second, as elections approach, parties serve as the central organizing locus for participation.

The transition period also marks the founding and re-birth of several new types of organizations; some organizations transform into new entities, others are resurrected from the past. In the case of Chile, new business associations, ethnic rights groups, and an environmental movement materialized. In almost all of the Latin American cases, pro-democracy organizations have surfaced during the transition to teach citizens about how and why to vote, what democracy is, and why their continued participation is important; these organizations often take on a voter registration project as well. Without fail, these groups have strong links to one or various political parties, or the state; the bulk of their funding comes from international sources. In Chile, the most influential of these organizations was *La Cruzada*, which after the plebescite vote became PARTICIPA; it was closely allied to the coalition of center and left parties called the *Concertación*.[28]

It was the combined pressure from organizations, parties and foreign governments, plus the internal dissent among elites that led the military regime to hold the plebescite and then the elections in Chile. With the victory of the NO in the 1988 plebescite and the triumph of the Christian Democrats in the 1989 elections, the seventeen year reign of authoritarianism came to an end. The Chilean case demonstrates that civil society can play a pivotal role in the breakdown of authoritarian rule. Civil society is often a key contributing factor in de-legitimizing and de-stabilizing an authoritarian regime; it does so by placing heavy demands upon the government and by attracting international attention to the abuses of the regime. However, an active civil society is not a necessary condition for a democratic transition to take place; democratization may occur without the impulse of citizens' organizations. This is most likely to occur in those transitions which are largely imposed from above or by an external actor.[29] As Schmitter (1993: 7) argues, associations and movements do not determine the timing, advent, or outcome of a regime transition, yet, they often do heavily influence the mode of the transition — whether it is through pushing for reform of the existing structure, through a revolutionary uprising, or by setting the stage and pressuring for a compromise or "pact" by between elite actors.[30] In most cases, civil society is a contributing factor, not the determining factor in the transition.

The role and influence of civil society and its distinct components have fluctuated over the past sixty years in Chile. Although the primary *raisons d'être* of civil society — to represent demands and meet needs of the citizenry — tend to remain the same after democratization, it is how those functions are fulfilled and by whom that change. This chapter has examined the particularities of the Chilean case, specifically, the function and influence of civil society under the prior democracy and also under authoritarian rule; in doing so, it allows us to understand better the organizations, their structures and their relationships with political parties in the contemporary period. As Chile now emerges from its transitional stage toward a consolidated democracy, questions arise as to what lessons the Chilean case yields about how a transition to democracy affects organized participation. Do the relationships of civil society return to their pre-authoritarian status, or do they adapt to their new environment? What incentives or constraints does such a change in political context place on citizens' organizations? Does democratization lead to a relative de-mobilization or a mobilization of civil society?

Notes

1. Pedro Jose Rubio Boldan, President of the *Sindicato de Hipodromo* Chile, and former President (1968–1973) of the Sindicato ECA y CORFO, interview with the author, July 16, 1994. For general historical background information on Chile and its social forces, see Petras and Leiva (1994), Petras (1970), and Whiting (1984).

2. In 1931, the Chilean military returned the power to rule back to civilians; in 1932, Arturo Alessandri was elected to the presidency, beginning a cycle of democratically elected rulers until the military coup ended Salvador Allende's term. The democracy had lasted forty-one years.

3. Cited in Valdés, 1993: 74.

4. The phenomena of participation booms in Chile parallels the experience of many other Latin American countries. See Elisabeth Friedman, "Women's Participation in Venezuela," Stanford University, unpublished MS 1995, for an excellent example; also Friedman (1998).

5. As a reflection of the foci of this book and related research constraints, this historical overview of civil society is limited mostly to participation in the urban centers, largely in Santiago, Chile. For information on organizing in rural and smaller urban areas, see June Nash et al (eds), *Popular Participation in Social Change*, The Hague: Mouton Publishers, 1976.

6. For more on labor organizing prior to 1973, see Frías (1993a and 1993b), Petras (1970) and Barrera and Falabella (1989).

7. For more on neighborhood councils under the prior democratic regime, see Vanderschueren (1971).

8. For more information on *Promoción Popular*, and on the *Juntas* and CEMAs under Frei, see Petras (1970, chapter 6) and Silva Donoso (1987, chapter 3).

9. See Chaney (1974) and Crummett (1977) for detailed overviews of the motivations and means of women's organizing under Allende.

10. See Chuchryk in Jaquette (1989) for more information.

11. There are various arguments as to why the breakdown occurred. In addition to rapid political mobilization, Whiting (1984) argues that three other factors contributed to the breakdown: external influences, economic conflict, and actions and attitudes of the party and government leaders. Valenzuela (1978) poses yet another approach: changes in the nature of politics itself (i.e. traditional rules and institutions) led to the breakdown. For a broad overview of the breakdown and overthrow of Chilean democracy see Sigmund (1977) and Valenzuela (1978).

12. Recall from Chapter 1 that herein political parties are defined apart from civil society (the collectivity of citizens' organizations).

13. This is, of course, not meant to imply that civil society is merely a phenomenon of the political left. On the contrary, citizens' organizations of the political right have played an important role in the development of civil society and during the transition to democracy.

14. Military coups are attempted for reasons of ethnic strife, economic turmoil or greed, corruption among leaders, disagreement on type of political system, desire for power, or factors internal to the armed forces. In Chile, the military-led coup of September 11, 1973 was intended to rid the country of "marxism" and progressive movements, and to implement a neo-liberal economic system. In the words of the four members of the military junta in a broadcast to the Chilean public on the morning of the eleventh, the coup was defined as being in response to "(1) the extremely grave social and moral crisis afflicting the country; (2) the inability of the government to control the chaos." The goal was "the liberation of the fatherland and to preclude our country from falling under the Marxist yoke, and the restoration of order and institutionality" (Broadcast on Radio Agricultura and Radio Minería; cited in Whelan, 1989: 455). For an overview of these possibilities, and an argument that factors internal to the military

56   *Beyond the Barricades*

(differences in training, education, political culture, and institutionalization) are often the instigators to a coup, see Arturo Valenzuela's "A Note on the Military and Social Science Theory," in *Third World Quarterly*, January 1985, pp. 132–143.

15.   It is important to note that the extent of the repression in Chile, although widespread, did not reach the proportions of other Latin American countries.   The "Report of the Commission on Truth and Reconciliation" records nearly 3,000 disappearances during the dictatorship; by contrast in El Salvador an estimated 75,000 were killed.

16.   Again, this overview of participation is not meant to be exhaustive; but instead it is meant to provide the context and background of organizations to be discussed in ensuing chapters.   For more on organizing under Chile's authoritarian regime, especially with regard to "popular" or grassroots organizations see Oxhorn (1995) and Schneider (1995).

17.   This process of re-birth may be somewhat easier in those countries which previously as well as recently had an active civil society under prior democratic rule.

18.   For an excellent argument of how authoritarianism can contribute to the democratization of civil society, see Oxhorn (1992 and 1995).

19.   As discussed by O'Donnell and Schmitter (1986), "hardliners" are those who wish to continue governing on their planned course, without making concessions to those who dissent and without liberalizing the political system.   The "softliners" advocate some opening or liberalizing of the political system.

20.   In 1983, the Confederation of Copper and Petroleum Workers united with four other union groups to form the CNT, which eventually gave way to become the CUT.   The CDT was born in 1984; it was originally formed as the *Grupo de los Diez* and passed on to be the Workers' Democratic Union (*Unión Democrática de Trabajadores*, UDT) before re-constituting itself as the CDT.

21.   Ruíz di Giorgio, as quoted in Barrera and Falabella (1989: 243).

22.   For more complete information on union organizing in Chile under authoritarianism, see Frías (1993) and Barrera and Falabella (1989).

23.   The singular best overview of the OEPs is Razeto et al (1990); excellent articles on OEPs by Roberto Urmeneta, Jaime del Pino and Margarita Fernandez appear in issues of *Economía y Trabajo*, Santiago: PET, 1991–1994. The most reliable source of statistics and analysis of the OEPs is the *Programa de Economía del Trabajo* (PET) in Santiago, Chile.

24. In the Chilean case, there was perhaps a third reason. In 1984, a plebescite vote was held so that citizens could decide whether or not Pinochet should stay in power. The YES vote won, amongst many accusations that there was fraud, that voters were ill-informed, and that citizens were too afraid to vote against the dictatorship. Either way, the loss at the polls played a role in the disillusionment and subsequent decrease in citizens' participation.

25. For a comprehensive overview of transitions toward democracy see O'Donnell and Schmitter, 1986.

26. The RN was comprised of the Democratic Independent Union (UDI), the National Union (UN), the National Labor Front, and the Social Christian Movement.

27. For an excellent discussion of the gap between electoralism and democracy, see Terry Karl's "Imposing Consent?: Electoralism versus Democratization in El Salvador," in *Elections in Latin America*, edited by Paul Drake and Eduardo Silva, Berkeley: University of California Press, 1986, pp. 9–36.

28. Parallel, although more conservative, organizations were CONCIENCIA in Argentina, CONCIENCIA in Peru, and LIBRA in Brazil. For more information on pro-democracy movements, especially those comprised of women, see Dorrit Marks (ed), *Women and Grass Roots Democracy in the Americas*, Miami: University of Miami, 1993; and Matear (1997).

29. Such was the case with the United States' involvement in Haiti's transition in 1994.

30. For a lengthy discussion on the modes and actors of transitions to democracy see, Terry Karl's "Dilemmas of Democratization in Latin America," *Comparative Politics*, Vol. 23, No. 1, October 1990, pp. 1–21.

CHAPTER THREE

Mobilization or De-Mobilization?

Participation Levels and Democratization

La historia cambió en 1990.
Lo que era no fue más y mucho
de lo que no era, nació. Unos
se aggiornaron y continuaron de
a caballo. Otros siguieron rígidos
y la montura se les arrancó.[1]

Pienso que estamos asistiendo a un
nacimiento y no a una defunción.[2]

Among theorists and politicians alike, there exists little consensus about what happens to organized participation following a transition to democracy. Whereas Huntington (1968) argues that democratization will likely lead to a participative boom, O'Donnell and Schmitter (1986) paradoxically suggest that participation will crest and diminish after a transition. This contradiction is present in the literature partially because scholars, embroiled in theoretical debates, have failed to do the most basic of tasks: count. Pateman asserts that "most theorists have been content to accept Sartori's assurance that the inactivity of the ordinary man is 'nobody's fault' and to take the facts as given for the purpose of theory building" (1970: 100). Yet without an actual tally of the varying number of organizations and participants over time, we cannot accept the inactivity of men and women as a given, much less assign blame for it. Therefore, while the ensuing chapters address the qualitative transformations of organizations, the objective of this chapter is to portray the quantitative changes in these groups and their memberships.[3] The results are somewhat incomplete but may prove surprising for some, since with the exception of women's identity (or feminist) groups, the numbers challenge the widely accepted assumption that organized participation declines significantly or disappears following democratization. This "headcount" of organizations over time serves as the first step toward understanding to what extent civil society will affect the quality, type and stability of the emerging democracies in Latin America.

DATA SAMPLE

How can one gauge levels of organized participation? This question is vital because how one measures participation is directly related to how one defines it. In this study there are three principal measurements, which when taken together, will be used to indicate the degree to which citizens participate in civil society: the numbers of organizations, their members, and activities. Therefore, organized participation is defined numerically in terms of collectivities, affiliation, and action. Ideally, participation should also be defined and measured in terms of the intensity of the activities, the influence of the organizations, and the commitment of the participants. But unfortunately, quantitative data for such indicators are not available for most of Latin American civil society; subsequent chapters in this study, however, do qualitatively address some of these issues.

Since this study focuses solely on group participation, data on individual participation (such as voting levels) will not be included. The sample herein is representative of the whole of civil society, although the actual examples are largely specific to the organizations which serve as the case studies for this research. Where data is not presented, it is because there is not sufficient information available. The special case of women's identity groups is discussed extensively in a later chapter, and should be viewed apart from all generalizations made within this chapter.

Where possible, data were collected for citizens' organizations under four periods: the prior democratic regime (corresponding to President Frei), the "socialist experiment" (Allende), authoritarian rule (Pinochet) and the emergent democracy (Aylwin and Frei). The most important data for this study are that comparing the levels of organized participation in the years immediately prior, during, and after the transition to democracy (approximately 1983-1994), since herein we are concerned with if and how participation levels change with re-democratization.

The reader should be forewarned that very little hard data are actually available about the levels of participation in Chilean civil society under the dictatorship versus under the contemporary democratic period. Therefore, many questions will remain unanswered. However, the data do allow us to establish that while in some areas participation somewhat diminishes, and in other realms it increases slightly, civil society does not demonstrate a significant trend either towards mobilization or de-mobilization following a transition back to democracy. There are even some cases in which the level of participation appears to be almost unaffected by re-democratization.

PROBLEMS IN MEASUREMENT

The evidence presented in this chapter should be taken more as an approximation of the changes in levels of organized participation than as an exact measurement. Precise and reliable measurements in this field are often impossible to obtain for several reasons. First, it is extremely difficult to collect data on organizations under authoritarian rule. Military rule instills fear in the populace and such fear leads citizens, and therefore organizations, to "cover their tracks." During the height of repression, most groups took protective measures and did not keep any membership records or meeting minutes. Opposition newspapers also protected clandestine organizations by not reporting about them or by not disclosing the names of participants; in other instances, they attempted to give more legitimacy to opposition forces by inflating their estimates of how many people attended protests and rallies. Therefore, most organizations did not keep records during the authoritarian period, and much of the documentation available is not entirely reliable as a source in itself.

A second challenge in measuring organized participation is that the only consistent source of data over time on organizations in Chile is the National Statistical Institute (INE). Yet statistics from the INE only count those organizations which have *personalidad jurídica*; this is the legal status that functional and territorial organizations obtain by registering their existence with the state. Many organizations rejected applying for such legal status under the military regime because they feared repression, anticipated no benefits, or because they perceived that requesting *personalidad jurídica* would be a legitimation of the dictatorship. Organizations could also be denied legal status because of their anti-military stance. Therefore, government records on participation levels do not depict the whole picture. It is likely that there were actually more organizations in existence during the 1980s than the total reported by the INE — how many more is unclear. Statistics compiled by CEN-PROS (the Center for Social Promotion and Research) indicate that the discrepancy between when organizations are founded and when they receive *personalidad jurídica* is insignificant among territorial organizations. It is only among functional organizations that there is a disparity between their moment of constitution and their procurement of legal status (see Appendices A and B for data charts). This is important to recall when looking at the "founding" rate of functional groups as reported by government statistics. Where possible, I have included data from other sources or from interviews with organizations' leaders to clarify any incongruities in the data.

Third, the method and level at which the state collects data on territorial organizations has been altered causing further problems in analyzing how organized participation has changed over the past twelve years. Prior to 1992, such data was collected on the national and regional levels, and compiled by the central government. Following the push toward municipalization in 1992, much of this data on organizations has been gathered by and recorded in the municipality. With 52 municipalities in Santiago alone, this new process renders data collection much more difficult for researchers; incongruous methods of data collection also present problems in comparing pre- and post-1992 statistics on territorial organizations.[4]

Finally, there is inevitably a selection bias towards groups which continue to survive; this is due to the obstacles involved in tracking the deaths of organizations. It is exceedingly difficult to locate past leaders of organizations which have disbanded, and to reconstruct accurately the life and death of a defunct group. There is also much uncertainty as to whether, how often, and how reliable data centers are about "cleaning" their lists — purging dead organizations from the roster. Much like the innumerable stories about people who have been dead for years but still receive pension checks or appear on voting registration lists, many organizations may continue to be counted long after they have ceased to function.

FUNCTIONAL ORGANIZATIONS

The data that are available indicate that functional organizations as a whole have not experienced a significant increase or decrease in the number of organizations, members or activities. Among our case studies, popular economic organizations (OEPs) and unions continue to persist following the transition back to democracy in Chile.

In 1973, Chilean labor unions were among the strongest in Latin America, numbering approximately 940,000 unionized workers and 6,692 unions. These numbers fell significantly in the ensuing decade due to the repressive policies of the military regime which prohibited many tools of labor organizing[5]; the decline is also attributable to the economic crisis of 1982, which crippled many of the industries in which unions were strongest. By 1987, union membership had fallen to 10% of the total workforce, from a Chilean high of 41% in 1972 (Chuchryk in Jaquette, 1989: 152). The 1994-1995 levels of unionism are comparable to the 1966-67 levels under the prior democratic regime of President Frei.

As demonstrated in figure 1 and figure 2, union growth rates climbed significantly during the period of the transition back to democracy, reaching levels of 13.8% and 15.6% in 1989 and 1991 respectively (Frías, 1993: 276-7). The reason for this increase is twofold. First, an opening of the political system initiated by Pinochet in the late 1980s allowed more space for citizens' participation; in particular, unions regained many of their rights to collective negotiation. Second, the re-born CUT (*Central Unitaria de Trabajadores*) held its first congresses in 1988 and 1991, providing a forum for

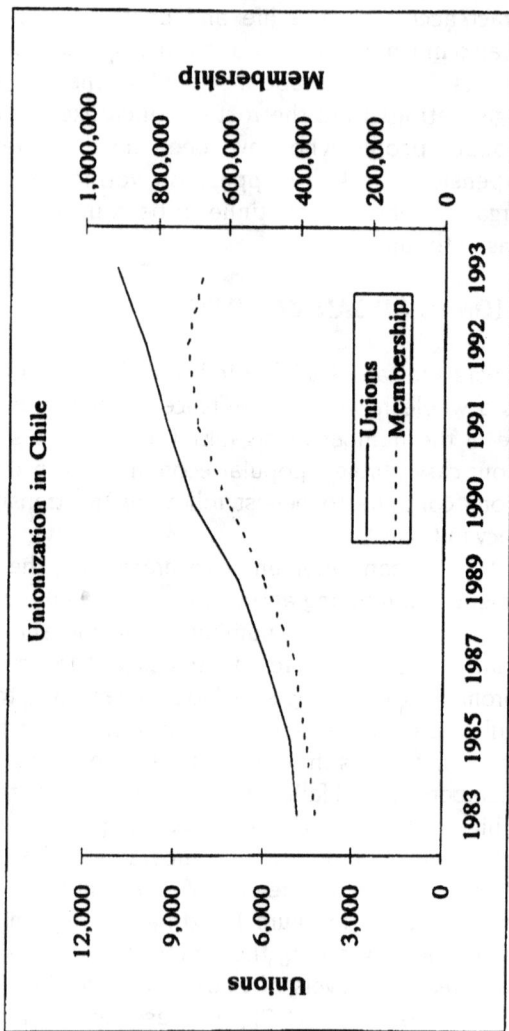

Figure 3.1[6]

Unionization in Chile

Figure 3.2[7]

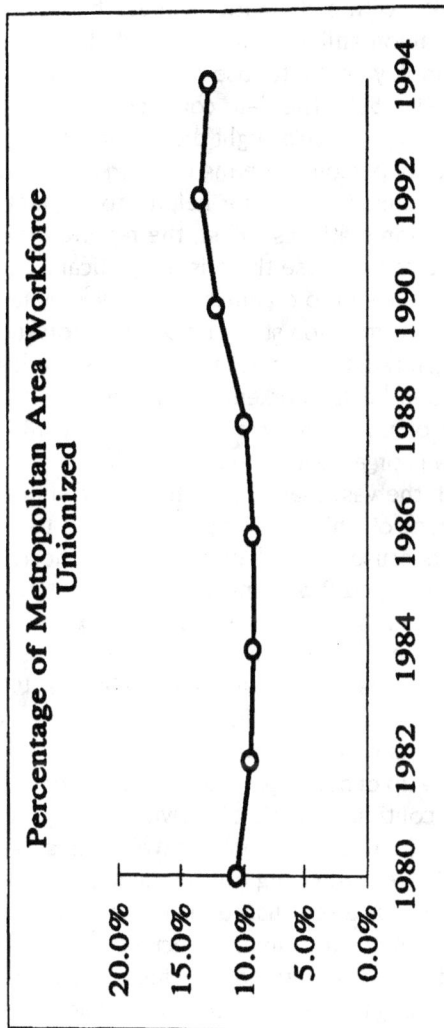

Percentage of Metropolitan Area Workforce
Unionized

unionists to make contacts, strategize, and gain publicity.[8] Note in the figures that the numbers of unions and affiliates increased through 1992, with a dramatic increase between 1989 and 1991. The rate of union affiliation grew by 7.8% between 1983 and 1993, while the employment rate rose by only 4.5% during the same period (Frías, 1994: 58). The data corresponding to unionization and membership experience a slight drop off in 1993, but still keep time with number of persons entering the workforce.

At this point, it would be helpful to highlight a few caveats about the union statistics. First, the reported levels of affiliation are a bit skewed because there is a significant number of workers that are not allowed to organize themselves by law. For example, in Chile, union affiliation statistics under-report the true number of workers organized; they do not include the extra-legal organizing of professors and health workers. Therefore, in 1992, when the supposed rate of unionism was 15.2%, actually 18.2 percent of the workforce was organized (Frias, 1993: 283).

Second, the vast majority of those workers not unionized say that their lack of union participation is due to the absence of a union, not because of a lack of volition. Of those polled, 52.3 percent of men and 52.9 percent of women say that the reason that they are not union members is that there exists no union for them to join; 28.9 percent of men and 29.1 percent of women attribute their non-participation to "no interest" (Guerra, 1994: 88). The former statistic, of course, implies great possibilities for the growth of Chilean unionism in the future.

In the realm of actual participation in union activities, the data also reveal continued levels of activity. As evidenced by figure 3, the number of strikes and workers involved in strikes rose throughout the 1980s, experiencing only a slight decline (or what may be considered a *bajón* as discussed in chapter 1) in 1993. The tremendous, but isolated surge, in union activity in 1991 is attributable to the coincidence of a national teachers' strike and a bus drivers' strike. According to Chilean union expert Patricio Frías, the level of union conflicts (including strikes and negotiations) has risen since 1989 due to the arrival of democracy (and the subsequent liberties extended to citizen organizing)[7]; but in contrast to the data on union and affiliation growth, the level of union activity is currently somewhat lower than during the previous democratic regime. For example, between 1966 and 1970 the (yearly average of the) total number of days workers were on strike (*días-huelga*) was 2,300,000; for 1991 it was 727,517. Like affiliation statistics, these statistics on strikes also appear to be on the increase, up from 87,451 in 1988 and 245,192 in 1990.[10]

Figure 3.3[11]

Union Strike Activity

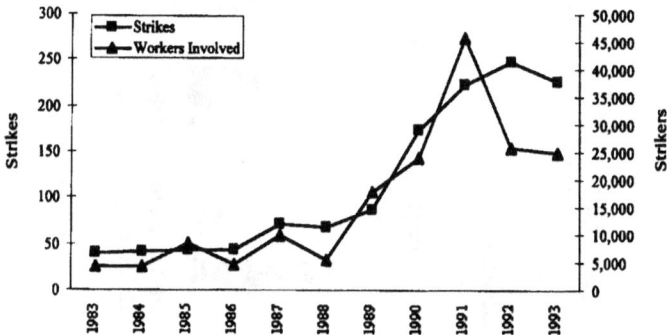

The statistics for participation in labor marches are much less reliable, but they do suggest that there has been a significant drop in the number of people attending such national level events. Figure 4 depicts the attendance estimations for May 1 (Labor Day) celebrations as reported on one the side by *El Mercurio* (the right-leaning, pro-military regime newspaper) and contrasted on the other side by the estimates of the opposition newspapers (*La Epoca, Fortín Mapocho, Solidaridad*). Both sets of estimates, however disparate they are from each other, indicate that there has occurred a steep decline in march attendance. It seems that while workers continue to belong to unions following re-democratization, their interest in national level acts and policies has waned; this trend is even more evident among those unions of the political left, which were highly politicized during the authoritarian period. Chapter 5 presents a qualitative argument (for which no quantitative data exists) that participation persists after the transition to democracy, but becomes much more local (or in this case, more union-specific).

Figure 3.4[12]

May 1 Celebration Attendance

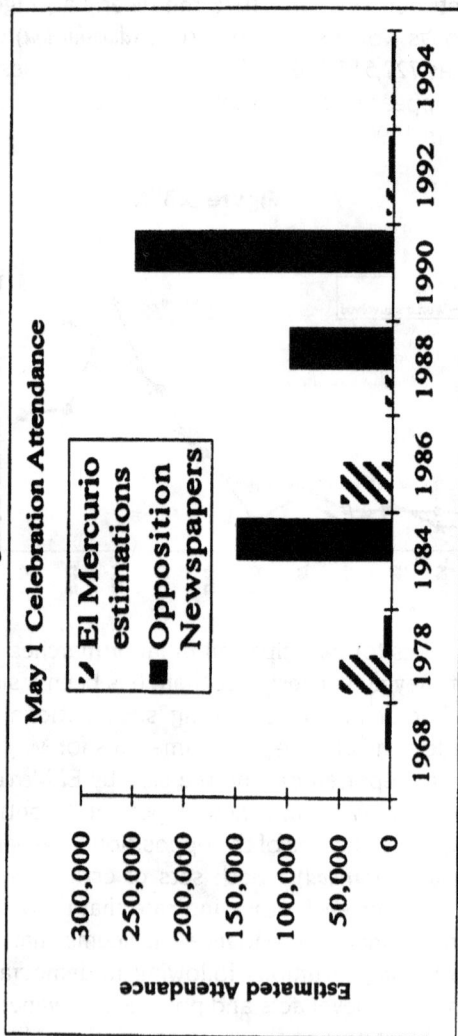

Figure 3.5[13]

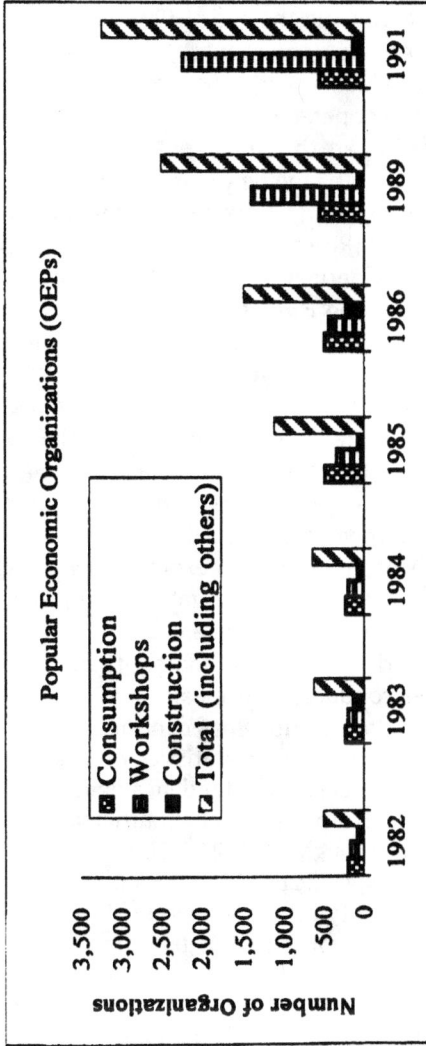

Popular Economic Organizations (OEPs)

Legend:
- Consumption
- Workshops
- Construction
- Total (including others)

Y-axis: Number of Organizations (0, 500, 1,000, 1,500, 2,000, 2,500, 3,000, 3,500)

X-axis: 1982, 1983, 1984, 1985, 1986, 1989, 1991

Organized participation in the form of Popular Economic Organizations (OEPs) also outlives the end of authoritarian rule in Chile. As demonstrated by figure 5, the total number of OEPs continued to rise throughout the end of 1991, led by the strength of the consumption groups (communal gardening groups and soup kitchens) and productive workshops (mostly craft guilds). It is only the construction cooperatives which have declined in number; this is perhaps due in part to the success of the government housing programs sponsored by the new democratic regime.[14] Of the OEPs included in Razeto's study, 84 percent of them were either growing or stable as of 1990 (Razeto, 1990: 210); the 1992 statistics from PET (Program on the Economics of Work, Chile) indicate that this trend is continuing. Among *Huertos* (communal gardening groups), the number of organizations decreased, while the number of participants increased by nearly ten percent between 1989 and 1992; this is because many of the groups merged their organizations and activities, while attracting new members. The *Comprando Juntos* (shopping cooperatives) initially decreased during the peak of the transition, but new organizations then began forming again (Allan, 1991: 15). The trajectory of health groups and common soup kitchens has been more stable, experiencing a slight rise in the number of participants and organizations. Artisan workshops have markedly increased; approximately 20 new workshops formed between 1989 and 1992.[15] Unfortunately, there has not been a census of the OEPs conducted since early 1992; it is therefore unclear if the number of organizations has continued to rise.

There exist no time-series statistics on the number of participants in OEPs. However, the attendance figures for FESOL (*Feria de la Económica Solidaria*) do suggest that participation in OEPs continued to be strong through 1994. FESOL is the annual fair begun in 1991 for OEPs —specifically for microenterprises, as well as for popular and solidarity organizations involved in economic development. In 1992, approximately 55,000 attended; in 1993 and 1994, that number rose and leveled off at an estimated 70,000.[16]

On a more general level, a 1994 survey polled organization leaders about the permanence of their level of activity over time by asking, "according to the objectives of your organization, have your activities been permanent over time, sporadic (sometimes on, sometimes off), or have there been prolonged periods of time in which it has not functioned?" Among functional organizations, 69.8% claim that their activities have been permanent over time, 14.1% view their activities as sporadic, and only 13.8% report that their organization has experienced prolonged breaks in activity.[17] Therefore, the great majority of organization leaders perceive that the activity levels of their membership have not dropped off during the initial stages of democratic consolidation.

The above case studies indicate that re-democratization does not lead functional organizations to experience a significant decline or escalation in numbers of groups or members. Groups persist despite the enormous changes in the political system and funding scenario. What remains indiscernible with the available data is the extent to which actual active participation within the functional groups subsides or sustains itself.

TERRITORIAL ORGANIZATIONS

The data for territorial organizations demonstrate more clearly a pattern of organizational resilience. The number of *Juntas de Vecinos* (neighborhood associations or councils) has continued to increase slightly and consistently during and after the transition to democracy (see figure 6). This is largely due to the fact that municipalization (the devolution of power to the local level) has opened new opportunities and funding possibilities for local organizations; also, under the new democracy, *Junta* leaders are now encouraged to give their input in some municipal decisions.[18] Meanwhile, actual participation levels within the *Juntas* themselves may have declined.

Under authoritarian rule in Chile, leaders of the neighborhood councils were appointed by the government; with the return to democracy, the leadership returned to be elected by the membership. Yet voting participation has been remarkably low. One study estimates that of the total population, only 20% are registered members of their neighborhood council, and only 40% of those members voted in the most recent *Junta* election (Gonzalez, 1994: 185). Several of the subjects interviewed for this study complained that although members did vote for *Junta* leaders, they did so with

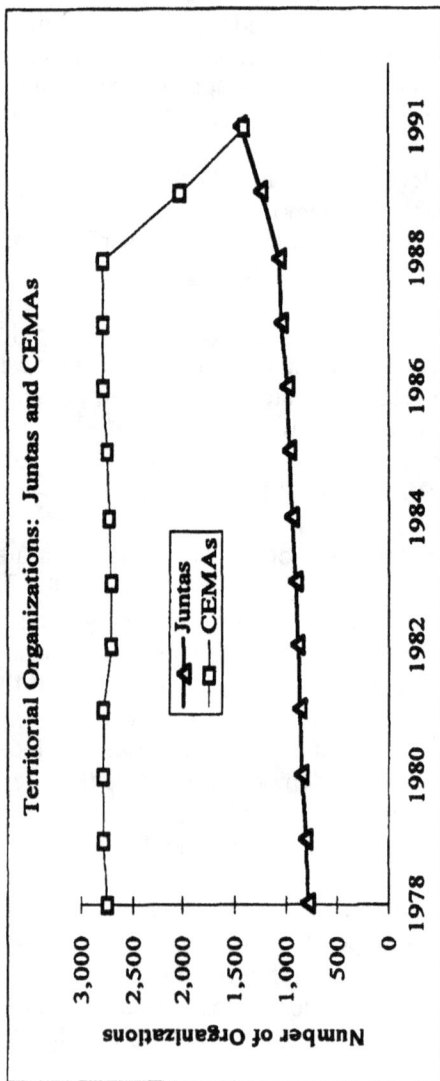

Figure 3.6[19]

Territorial Organizations: Juntas and CEMAs

very little knowledge of the candidates' platform or ideology. No additional data could be found to shed light on participation levels among *Junta* members. However, as mentioned above, one survey polled organization leaders about the permanence of their level of activity over time. Among territorial organizations (including neighborhood councils), 50.4% claim that the quantity and intensity of their activities have been permanent over time, 26.9% view their activities as sporadic, and 21.2% report that the organization has experienced prolonged breaks in activity.[20] If not among the *Juntas*, in which territorial groups do citizens continue to participate? As figure 7 and figure 8 indicate, much of the participatory impulse of citizens may have been channeled into other territorial organizations since the return to democracy. Community cultural, sports, and non-classified organizations have multiplied at an astounding rate (the latter span the realm of senior citizens' clubs, day-care cooperatives, micro-enterprises, craft centers, and support groups, among others). With the end of the highly politicized period of authoritarian rule, citizens may have more time or desire to focus on non-political activities. According to the Director of Community Development for Lo Espejo, many of those participating in these types of territorial organizations have not taken part in community activities since the prior democracy. She believes that

FIGURE 3.7[21]

Sports Clubs

Figure 3.8[22]

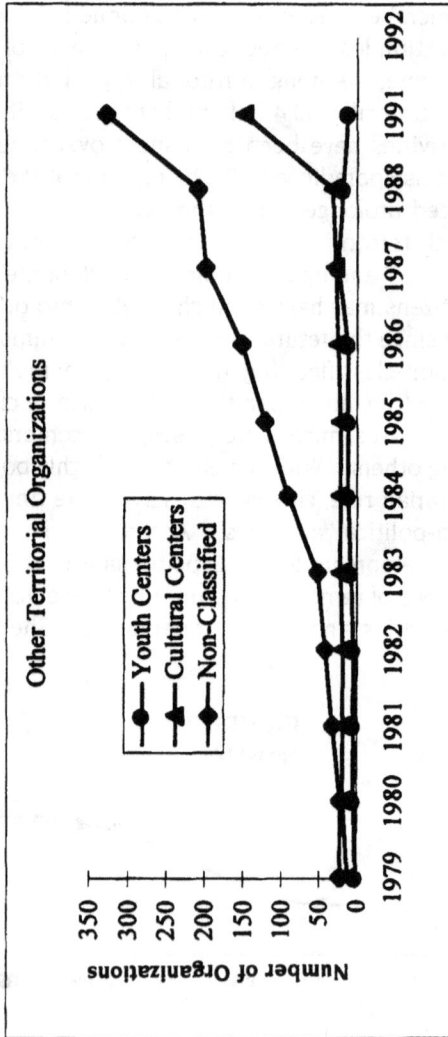

Other Territorial Organizations

Legend:
- Youth Centers
- Cultural Centers
- Non-Classified

Y-axis: Number of Organizations (0, 50, 100, 150, 200, 250, 300, 350)

X-axis: 1979, 1980, 1981, 1982, 1983, 1984, 1985, 1986, 1987, 1988, 1991, 1992

their re-entry into civil society through cultural and athletic groups signals their fear of political participation — reflective either of their fear of de-railing the democracy with too much participatory pressure (as under Allende), or their fear of repression (a vestige of the Pinochet years).[23] Nonetheless, participation in territorial organizations strongly persists, and in some realms (especially in the sports and cultural arenas) even mobilizes, following re-democratization. The one exception to this is the CEMAs (mothers' centers).[24]

CEMA-Chile was founded in the early 1960s, by the state, to organize neighborhood women to learn skills which would be useful in the household. It evolved into an organization which taught women how to supplement their household income while remaining in the home, as well as a vehicle for encouraging women to maintain traditional gender roles and foster family values. It quickly grew into the largest citizens' organization in Chile. By 1974, there were approximately 20,000 CEMAs with nearly one million members. Yet in 1982 that number had dropped to 9,061 centers with 230,000 members (Valdés, 1993a: 99). These numbers have continued to decrease slightly, even during the height of organizational mobilization in the 1980s; with the emergence of new women's organizations, some members abandoned CEMA. The sum total of CEMAs has now decreased beyond that of the democratic regime under Frei; in 1966 there were 3,000 CEMAs in Santiago and 2,500 in the provinces with an average of 50 members each (Valdés, 1993a: 56).

As evidenced by figure 6 above, a significant decline in CEMAs occurred between 1990 and 1992. This is because CEMA has always been directed by the President's wife; the organization thus became highly linked with the military regime under the directorship of Lucía Hiriat de Pinochet during the 1970s and 1980s. When the authoritarian regime lost legitimacy, CEMA too lost legitimacy — and members. As a way of rejecting the Pinochet government, the emerging democratic regime instead chose to support women's organizing through the inception of a new state agency, SERNAM (the National Women's Service), and thereby drastically reduced the state resources available to CEMA-Chile. SERNAM may not only have aided in the reduction of CEMA, but as discussed in

Chapter 6, it may also have been a contributing factor in the demobilization of an entire category of organizations: women's identity groups.

GENERALIZING ABOUT ORGANIZATIONAL RESILIENCE

With the exception of women's identity groups, whose special case will be discussed in a later chapter, what can be said with certainty is that there continue to exist organizations and participants within Chilean civil society after the transition to democracy. The mass disbanding of organizations, as predicted by some, has not occurred. Yet due to insufficient data available, one cannot be conclusive about whether there is more or less intensity and commitment of the citizenry to participate following re-democratization. It is also unclear whether the data which indicate that organizations have survived the transition actually reflect a continued participation of the same groups and individuals, or if the data hide the deaths of some organizations which have in turn been replaced by the births of others.

Although many organizations *persist* following re-democratization, transitions to democracy may *discourage* the emergence of new organizations. This lower rate of organizational foundings will be due to three reasons. First, there may be an assumption by citizens that political interests are represented in a democracy, and therefore non-governmental organization is not necessary. Second, new organizations will have to compete with political parties and established organizations for resources, membership, and publicity. Finally, the most expensive stage for organizations is the founding; and after re-democratization, there is a decided lack of funding available for organizational maintenance or start-up costs. Therefore, new organizations are not likely to emerge in great numbers immediately following a transition back to democracy.

Either way, the evidence does indicate that both Huntington, and O'Donnell and Schmitter were mistaken. A transition back to democracy yields neither a boom nor a significant diminution in participation. In Chile, organized participation seems to have survived re-democratization. In fact, in some cases, the *level* of participation appears to have been almost unaffected by the enormous changes which occurred in the Chilean political system; it is instead the *type* of participation which has been altered.[25] Transformations have occurred in and among organizations, and our studies of those groups must reflect such transformations. Those scholars researching participation levels must put on new eyeglasses, or search different corners, in order to find the emergent forms of participation under democracy in Latin America. As the director of an umbrella organization for OEPs explained, organizations are "like kids — they go through a stage where you think they have disappeared — they're not in school or in the house like before, but they can be found in other places, in different places. It's where you look..."[26] The following two chapters examine where and how these organizations transformed in order to survive the transition back to democracy.

Notes

1.   As this quotation does not translate easily, I have left it in its original Spanish. An approximate translation would be: "History changed in 1990. That which existed ceased to exist, and much of what did not exist was born. Some adapted to the ride and continued on horseback. Others rode rigidly and the saddle got away from them (or, they fell off the saddle)." Sara Vásquez, president of the national federation of *ollas comunes*, as quoted in El Mercurio, "*Ollas comunes cambian giro: se convierten en microempresas*," November 1992.

2.   Guillermo Campero (1993: 29). Translated, it means "I think that we are attending a birth and not a death."

3.   In organization theory, this approach is known as "population ecology" which predicts deaths over births of organizations, discusses organizational survival, and the importance of the environment in studying populations of organizations. Under this model, the hallmark of success is seen as survival and adaptation of organizations through a process of selection. See Carroll (1984) and Hannan and Freeman (1977, 1989).

4.   For example, the sample size, geographic boundaries, and census methods differ.

5.   Such as collective negotiation and strikes; see chapter 2 for more details on how union activity was repressed under authoritarian rule in Chile. In the case of El Salvador, the experience of unions and democratization is much more complex; see Fitzsimmons and Anner (1999).

6.   Source: PET, compiled from statistics from the *Dirección del Trabajo*, Santiago, Chile.

7.   Source: PET, compiled from statistics from the *Dirección del Trabajo*, Santiago, Chile.

8.   With the arrival of the democratic regime, the CUT was able to hold its first national congress in October of 1991. I focus on the CUT in this study because it is the strongest labor organization in Chile, representing 12.6% of the workforce in the country (See Frías, 1993).

9.   Under the authoritarian regime, many unions were not associated with a firm that had the right to negotiate; that fact likely explains at least some of the increase in union conflicts under the emergent democracy.

10.   For the reporting of these statistics and for more extensive data comparing the previous democratic regime to the authoritarian period in Chile, see Frías (1992: 19-23).

11.   Source: As cited in Patricio Frías, "*Sindicatos en la transición*," in *Economía y Trabajo en Chile*, 1993-1994, p. 63.

12.   As compiled by author from newspaper accounts in *El Mercurio*, *La Epoca*, and *Fortín Mapocho*.

13.   Source: Statistics compiled from PET (Catastro, 1992) and Quiñones (1994: 39).

14.   The program began under President Aylwin in 1990 through the Ministry of Housing, directed by Minister Alberto Etchegaray.

15.   The best data available for past and present OEPs are at PET (*Programa de Economía del Trabajo*), where I spent much time researching; some information is also available in Schild (1992), Allan (1991), and Razeto (1990).

16.   See publication "*Microempresa*," Santiago: PET, January 1994, p. 14 and January 1995, p. 12.

17.   As reported in CENPROS, 1994: question 25. Of those polled, 2.3% responded "don't know/no answer."

18.   This, of course, varies according to the municipality and the volition of the governing elected officials.

19.   Source: Compiled by author from data from the *Compendio Estadístico, Instituto Nacional de Estadístias*, Santiago, Chile.

20.   As reported in CENPROS, 1994: question 25. 1.4% of those polled responded "don't know/no answer."

21.   Source: Compiled by author from data from the *Compendio Estadístico, Instituto Nacional de Estadística*, Santiago, Chile.

22.   Source: Compiled by author from data from the *Compendio Estadístico, Instituto Nacional de Estadística*, Santiago, Chile.

23.   Author's interview with Elena Vergen, Department of Community Development, Comuna de Lo Espejo, Santiago de Chile, July 25, 1992.

24.   Under *Diario Oficial* Law #16.880 (August 7, 1968), CEMAs were first defined as functional organizations.   Although they were considered autonomous community organizations along with *Juntas* and sports clubs, the Mothers' Centers depended upon the government founded CEMA-Chile Foundation. *Diario Oficial* Law #18.893 (December 30, 1989) replaced Law #16.880, changing the status of CEMAs to be defined as territorial organizations.

25.   As one researcher explains in reference to OEPs, "The mechanical interpretation of a strong decrease in organizations has not been verified. Instead, one observes processes of re-grouping and development along with challenges and tendencies that evolve them in diverse directions" (Allan, 1991: 29).

26.   Winnie Lira, director of the Fundación Solidaridad, interview with the author on August 3, 1994.

CHAPTER FOUR

Organizational Transformation:
Taking Politics Out of Democracy

No estoy ni ahí
con la política.[1]

Yesterday for Democracy,
Today for Dignity.[2]

The 1970's and 1980's were decades during which citizens mobilized around political issues in Chile. Workers protested for and against state nationalization programs; women rallied in opposition to human rights abuses of the military. Politics was a focal point for the participation of individuals in an entire spectrum of organizations. Neighborhood associations tried to influence municipal budgeting, sustenance groups clamored for their demands to be included in political party platforms, and Catholic Church organizations sought to reverse government positions on human rights issues. Innumerable organizations called for greater opportunities for participation in government decisions and policies; citizens demanded "government by the people."

Yet for most sectors of civil society, this drastic change in environment — a transition back to democracy — has caused organizations and their members to adapt in ways which have led them far away from the political realm. Political activity has significantly fallen off since the dizzying days of the transition when political mobilization and organization were at an all time high. This argu-

ment that de-politicization occurs following a transition is nothing
new; it has been posited by O'Donnell and Schmitter (1986), and
Canel (1993), among others. Many of them claim that as a government ends the repression and stops actively interfering in the lives
of citizens, it is natural that the citizens will cease viewing the government as the primary target of their activity. Others, such as
Schneider (1995) and Oxhorn (1995), suggest that the new democratic regime in Chile favored traditional partisan representation
over popular organizing. And in his very provactive essay, Moulian
argues that "the most premeditated manifestation of forgetting is
de-politicization," in the Chilean case, de-politicization was facilitated by a transformation of the culture from one that valued solidarity to one based on competitive individualism (Moulian, 1998:
20). Yet most references to de-politicization by politicians and
scholars have only been in the form of an hypothesis or casual
observation. This chapter, therefore, is an attempt to build upon
this discussion by demonstrating how and to what extent de-politicization manifests itself, what activities fall by the wayside, what
replaces them, and why this phenomenon occurs. It represents an
assertion and documentation of the existence of de-politicization
as one aspect of organizational transformation after a change in
political context from authoritarianism to democracy. It is, in fact,
the most important type of organizational transformation since its
scope and potential to affect change are much greater than the
other aspects of transformation. I refrain from placing a value judg-
ment on the de-politicization phenomenon; however, the implications of it and its effect on democratic consolidation will be discussed in the concluding chapters.

    With the dawn of democratic consolidation, citizens and organi-
zations throughout civil society tend to channel their participation
and energies to realms other than the political. The following
anecdote captures this de-politicization, as recounted by the director of a foundation working with women's sustenance groups and
confirmed by the participating women:

> When we were invited to do an exposition in New York, I talked with the
> Chilean Consul who showed me an arpillera (an artcraft between needlepoint
> and quilting) he had. It was a small one, showing a rainbow, with lots of

pobladores underneath it holding banners that said things like "happiness is here" and "welcome democracy." It really was an exciting piece of work — even the cars depicted had little signs that said "beep, beep" to let you know that everything was working. So the Consul and I decided to start the exposition with an enormous replica of that arpillera hailing in democracy; we would hang it over the doorway and then the exposition could tell the story from the beginning.

So, I looked at the back of the arpillera to see which taller (organizational workshop) had made it (it is always marked on the back). And I went to meet with the women to tell them about the project. Well, I explained everything to them. They sat and listened. I talked about how exciting this project was and how proud we all were to participate in it. They just sat there like this (chin resting on hands, no expression or motion). I told them how much the Consul liked their work. Then they said nothing, and so I said, is someone going to tell me what is going on?

They said that they would do any arpillera except that one — they didn't believe all those things about democracy anymore. All of those wonderful things that were supposed to come with democracy, didn't appear. So, they were willing to do an arpillera on any other theme like recycling, the environment, or domestic abuse, but not on that theme, not on democracy.

So, I said to them, if one of your children was going through a bad time, does that mean you wouldn't tell the wonderful story of their birth, and keep the hope that things will get better?

They did the arpillera — it ended up so beautiful — and they said that in making it, it brought them much happiness and hope.[3]

This quotation illustrates three crucial points. First, as demonstrated in Chapter 3, organizations do not disband after a transition to democracy; participation continues throughout civil society Second, many citizens experience a disillusionment with democracy after the initial transition. Third and most applicable to this chapter, citizens change the foci and expressions of their participation. At one time, it was commonplace for the women of this workshop to make arpilleras addressing the political situation of their country, often by expressing their disdain for repression or aspiration for democracy. Currently, although many women continue to produce artcrafts, their messages are no longer directed at the country's leaders, institutions or type of governance. New topics, more focused on territorial, cultural, economic or family issues are now dominant. The desire of these women to participate, but in realms other than the political, is exemplary of a general trend that has pervaded civil society in Chile since the return to democratic rule.

POLITICAL PARTICIPATION UNDER DEMOCRACY

It is arguable whether participation of the citizenry, or merely the opportunity to participate, is a necessary condition for the existence of democracy. This theoretical debate, along with the dispute over whether participation is de-stabilizing to democracy, was already explored in Chapter 1. What remained unfinished in the discussion, were the possible roles and effects of participation under democracy.[4] First, participation may positively or negatively affect the economic well-being of individual citizens, a neighborhood, or even of the government. Perhaps the best example of this is how the trucking unions paralyzed the Chilean economy in 1973 under Allende with their general strike. Protesting inflation, the lowering of wages, and nationalization programs, the truckers managed to impede significantly national trade and transportation. On a more local level, since the resources of the state are minimal, functional organizations can aid individuals in the lower-income classes in overcoming poverty by teaching skills or supplementing food and income levels, such as in the cases of adult literacy programs or common soup kitchens.

Second, participation influences the level of social conflict; in extreme cases, it may lead to violence or the de-stabilization of democracy. Some might argue that the social division caused by exorbitant levels of participation of the citizenry under the years of Allende was a primary cause of the breakdown of Chilean democracy; instead of promoting solutions and unity, participation might be viewed as having fomented divisiveness and excessive pressure on the government leading to instability. Or alternatively, participation may channel conflict negotiation among factions, forcing individuals and groups to confront their problems as in the case of collective bargaining between unions and firms or public debates regarding neighborhood land use.

A third function of participation under democracy is its effect on individual dignity and self-worth. Under a dictatorship much of society may be dependent upon the state; citizens may be stripped of many of their participatory options, their right to congregate, and the ability to influence government decisions. In the more extreme case of a totalitarian state, the government may pervade virtually all aspects of an individual's life. Conversely, participation in an emerging democracy can encourage citizens to make decisions, learn skills, develop identity/ies, find a community, and be independent — whether it be of the state or of a spouse.

A fourth role of participation is that citizens' participation may affect, in an adverse or beneficial manner, government policies or state institutions. For example, as Chile continues its program of de-centralizing the government, what happens to participation on the local level will be very important to the success or failure of the program. Citizens may choose to bypass the municipality in favor of relations with national institutions or transnational actors thereby hampering the potential effects of de-centralization; or they may choose to participate in the opportunities presented within the municipality, which would bolster and legitimize the de-centralization process. Participation of the citizenry may also be pivotal in electing or blocking a candidate or political party for office, lobbying for a specific policy, or proposing reforms to the justice system.

In most transitions (back) to democracy, certainly in every Latin American transition during the last two decades including those of Argentina, Brazil and Uruguay, all four roles of participation have been activated by the citizenry. Yet, the fourth function of participation will often cease, at least momentarily, following the completion of that transition if a country subsequently enters into a phase of democratic consolidation. This is the case in Chile, where the focal point of civil society is becoming significantly less political.

At this point, a definition of how "political" is used in this book would be appropriate. Herein, "political" shall be limited only to that which is directly related to government policy, type, actions, elections, or institutions. Therefore, when I argue that the focal point of an organization has diverged from the political realm, it means that the group is no longer focusing its energies, resources and time on government, state or regime-related issues. When this is the case with a majority of the organizations, civil society may be said to be withdrawing from politics.

There exists a large body of literature which posits that what was once relegated to the "personal" realm may also be considered as "political." Most notable is the work of Marysa Navarro who argues that the Argentine Mothers of the Plaza de Mayo (mothers of the disappeared) have successfully re-defined and expanded the realm of the political to include matters of the family, gender and household.[5] It is not my intention to enter into this discussion, or to imply that issues of the environment, gender relations, family or poverty should not ever be considered political; nor do I mean to intimate that civil society is retreating from these issues. Such issues dealing with relationships of power, authority, and designated responsibility would clearly fall under any broad definition of "political," and groups certainly continue to mobilize around these issues. Yet for the sake of theoretical rigor and clarity in this project (and for lack of a more appropriate or precise term), "political" shall be used in its narrow, more traditional definition of that which relates to the government, state or regime.

Why stick with the potentially confusing term "political" in lieu of substituting a different or new word? First, "de-governmentalization" might have replaced "de-politicization," except that the latter is also intended to apply to situations in which the focus may be not the government, but the type or medium of governance. The former term is limited to the government. Second, I have also chosen to continue employing the word "de-politicization" for the sake of theoretical continuity. As stated above, this chapter builds upon the earlier work of theorists such as O'Donnell and Schmitter who refer to "the de-politicization of civil society"; substituting another word now might help to evade confusion within this particular work, but would only serve to add another layer to the taxonomical clutter of the discipline. Therefore, I will continue to refer to the phenomenon at hand as "de-politicization."

It is also important to underscore that under authoritarian rule political symbolism abounds; almost everything may be construed as a symbol of the resistance or in support of the military regime. This is because with all political power vested in one faction, society becomes highly politicized. Under authoritarianism, one is either for or against the dictatorship; in an attempt to facilitate methods of control, little room is left for fence-sitters. By definition, under a democratic regime there is more leeway for loyal dissension. Since the government does not interfere in so many aspects of life, democracies (with the exception of crisis situations) are usually significantly less politicized. Therefore, under authoritarianism, a lack of food or housing may be depicted by opposition organizations as a systematic attempt by the dictatorship to further marginalize its opposition; or pro-government groups may accuse union workers on strike for higher wages of trying to immobilize the economy in order to bring down the regime. Everything can be given a political connotation. Yet after a transition (back) to democracy, although many of the activities are basically the same, the emphasis and symbolism of organizations' actions may change. In the case of Chile, political symbolism is now often avoided, and activities aimed at the central government take a decidedly backseat. How widespread is this de-politicization effect? After examining the breadth of this phenomenon, this chapter surveys how de-politicization manifests itself and finally, why it transpires.

THE DE-POLITICIZATION OF ORGANIZATIONS

On the general level of civil society, outside the realm of political parties, my field research yielded few examples of organizations that are unaffected by the de-politicization phenomenon. By definition, parties will continue to be political, functioning within the domain of elections and governmental policy. Yet other organizations are rapidly withdrawing from the political arena, and nonpolitical groups are surpassing the traditionally political associations in numbers of organizations, members and activities. Contrary to the Pinochet years, the more highly political organizations (such as human rights groups and pro-democracy associations) are no longer the fastest growing organizations in Chile. Although no statistics are available on the two former groups, it is widely agreed among Chilean leaders and organizers that the growth rate for human rights groups is flat, and pro-democracy movements have also peaked and may be in decline.[6] It is the decidedly non-political organizations like sports clubs, youth centers, cultural groups, senior citizen organizations, and micro-enterprises that boast the highest growth rates in the 1990s.[7] Most dramatically, in the four year period between 1988 and 1992, the number of cultural/artistic organizations more than tripled, and youth groups expanded to two and a half times their previous number.[8] Overall, for that same period throughout Chile, the number of (non-political) community and functional organizations increased by 28.5 percent.

On the level of the individual, there are no statistics available that allow for a measurement of (de-)politicization over time in Chile. In most Latin American countries, one might look at the level of voter participation. However, in Chile voting is obligatory; therefore, voting statistics tell us only that almost all Chileans are law-abiding citizens and thus go to the polls. There are very few opinion surveys which measure the politicization of citizens, defined apart from partisanship. One found that Chileans are rapidly turning away from political parties; the percentage of those not identifying with a party rose from 22% in June 1990 to 34% in July 1991. Eighty-seven percent of those surveyed claimed not to participate in politics, while 71% expressed little or no interest in politics.[9] Another polled citizens on four questions: "how much do you watch political forums/advertisements and debates on television? do you read about politics in the newspapers? do you talk about politics in your family? do you talk about politics with your friends?" In 1993, just prior to the presidential elections, 44 percent of the population reported never or almost never doing any of the above; 36.6% did them occasionally and only 19.4% claimed to do so with frequency. Unfortunately, these statistics are static, since polling on these questions did not begin until 1992. However, in the same poll just prior to the 1989 elections, citizens were asked how often they watched the candidates' television advertisements (*franjas*); 38% reported to watch them everyday or nearly everyday. In 1993, just 18.5% did so. Significantly fewer Chilean citizens watched politically-related elections programming in 1999 and 1993 as compared to 1989.[10]

Among organizations, it is the groups that were most highly politicized throughout the transition period that now show marked patterns of de-politicization — a phenomenon most notable among functional organizations. As in the previous chapter, we will examine the same set of cases, which are a representative sample of the whole of civil society. The indicators used to measure the level of politicization vary between each organization; that is because the indicator that yields the most accurate depiction of the politicization of one group, may not exist in a measurable form for another group. For example, there is just one single publication that has represented the Popular Economic Organizations (OEPs) over time; its editorials may thus serve as an indicator of the major issues which have concerned and motivated the members of the OEPs. On the other hand, there are numerous publications which have come out of the feminist movement, some out-lasting others, and each representing a different feminist organization or inclination; taking an accurate measurement on such a diverse sample is extraordinarily difficult. Therefore, another indicator is applied to gauge the politicization of identity organizations; in this case, it is the symbolism reflected in their chants and marches.

Once again, under the realm of functional organizations we examine the cases of OEPs and unions. OEPs have never been exceedingly political organizations; their primary reason to organize has always been economic, with politics and identity as secondary motivations. However, during the height of authoritarian rule, the OEPs participated overtly in the political realm; the relative importance of political issues to these organizations has since decreased significantly. This is evident in the names they adopt, their publication, and their activities. The names that OEPs choose range from those that reflect religious conviction (*Taller San Francisco*) or political positions (*Ollas Libertad*) to those that reveal the location (*Coordinadora Talagante*) or activity (*Coordinadora Arpilleristas*) of the organization. Depending upon the group, names are chosen either by consensus of the membership or by designation of the founding member. Either way, an organization's name is reflective of the immediate concerns and/or planned activities of the members at the time of founding. For example, a proportionately higher percentage of OEPs were christened with religious names around the time of the Pope's visit to Chile in the early 1980s — a period in which religious sentiments and professions in the country were running at an all-time high. Likewise, analyzing the name given to organizations at their time of founding should give some indication of the level of politicization of the groups and their members. According to Razeto et al (1990: 216), a significantly higher proportion of OEPs selected politically-oriented names in the period between 1973 and 1982, compared to the following eight year period. This trend continues even more dramatically in the years since the inauguration of the democratic regime. The few OEPs that have been founded since 1990 have, without known exception, taken names which contain no explicit reference to politics; instead, they have chosen names reflective of their function as workshops, gardening groups, etc.[11] Explains Maria Paz, "the name of our organization is as important to our identity, our being (*ser*), as the name of each of us (individuals) is."[12] As the identity of the OEPs as a whole changes, so too do the names chosen by the newly emergent organizations.

Another indication of the level of politicization of OEPs is *La Hoja*, the only magazine in Chile devoted entirely to news and issues related to the OEPs. *La Hoja* was first published in 1982, and is now in circulation six to seven times per year. A review of the issues from 1987 to the present shows that over 70 percent of the issues in the period between 1987 and 1989 have editorials referring to the struggle for democracy, the OEPs' role under such a regime, and the suffering the people endured under military rule. For example, in 1988 (issue 49) the editors write, "a democracy that does not pay attention to popular participation, will not have much content...popular organization must not only be taken into account, but it must be a pillar of the process...our repression must end," and in 1989 (issue 52), "after living through so much misery and repression, the OEPs have to give much support in the future democracy." Since 1991, such commentaries have remained almost entirely absent from the editorial pages — only 28 percent of the editorials now discuss political issues. In fact, the only references to politics are those concerning governmental funding agencies, and two editorial commentaries related to the elections. Most editorials now discuss the need for members to acquire better accounting skills, or the importance of establishing rules and budgets within each organization. Although OEPs never reached a high level of politicization, a macro-view of their organizations' names and publication demonstrates that their discourse is certainly less political now than during the height of the transition back to democracy. The form and sequencing of such de-politicization are captured in the following micro-studies of two OEPs.

In the final years of the transition, the organizations of *Talleres Genesis* concentrated on producing and selling their artisan crafts (*arpilleras*, pillow covers, and purses), the great majority of which incorporated pictures or slogans denouncing the military regime or glorifying democracy.[13] Members would also support the party or candidate of their choice (although, "we were almost all for the same side, so we organized together"), attend political rallies together, and invite candidates or party officials to give talks at their weekly meetings. The coordinators also organized the members to make banners to carry in the political rallies and protests which read, for example, "NO to hunger, NO to Pinochet" and "Democracy, now!" With the advent of the long-awaited democracy, *Talleres Genesis* continue to devote the majority of their efforts to artisan products; these products, however, no longer make reference to the type of governance. Instead, they focus on community life, health issues, or the environment. Meetings now focus on preparing for craft fairs, and include seminars on design, family relations and accounting. Participation in political rallies and marches has fallen by the wayside; the organization limits itself to one or two political forums per year. As Tina, one of the *Genesis* coordinators explains, "We women, we used to be against Pinochet. But now in these times, most of us are indifferent to politics. We concern ourselves more about the problems of our children and community than the silly little problems of the government."[14]

Throughout the late 1980s, the activities of *Talleres Melipilla* also reflected the highly politicized environment in which they functioned. Like many of the *talleres*, their internal structure consisted of several committees, one of which was the *Comité Revindicativo*. This committee focused on presenting demands and connecting the organization's economic goals with the opposition's struggle to oust Pinochet. Yet since the end of military rule, *Talleres Melipilla* have put aside their political activities to focus on various other concerns. In addition to their continued production of artisan goods, they now have the following committees:

Development, researches and plans for those areas where there is a need (in the realm of production).

Pro-glasses (*pro-anteojo*), *Talleres Melipilla* made an agreement with their local Lions Club that their members would do the community collection (door-to-door) for the Lions if they would donate eyeglasses for the women of the *talleres* in the community.

Health, addresses the health concerns of the members and their children through forums, educational talks, and financial support in emergency situations.

Recreation, plans two trips a year for the enjoyment and solidarity of members.

Revindicativo is no longer a functioning committee within *Talleres Melipilla*. As one of the members explained to me, "No *estamos ni ahí con la política*" — which is a common, idiomatic expression in Chile. Roughly translated, it means "We're not into politics", and is now frequently uttered by those who claim always to have been a-political, as well as those who profess to be tired or disillusioned with political causes and crises. "No *estoy ni ahí con la política*" might be considered the unofficial motto these days of many students and unionists — as well as taxi drivers, who under the final years of Pinochet were likely to open the floodgates of their political opinions to any unsuspecting passenger who happened to ask them, "so how are things going?" *Talleres Genesis* and *Talleres Melipilla* are concrete examples of the greater general trend among OEPs to depoliticize following a transition to democracy.

In regards to another type of functional organization, Campero and Cortazar (1988: 125) argue that there are three primary objectives for unions: socio-economic, organizational, and political. The former are the socio-economic advantages that can be gained for its members. The second are the benefits for the organization itself and its leaders. The political objectives are those related to the functioning of the socio-economic or political system. I would argue that following the transition to democracy, unions have maintained only the first two objectives. As discussed in Chapter 5, union organizing has become much more localized and individualistic. Although unionists do retain an active interest in the economic system — more as a barometer of their employment than as a policy objective — union organizing has also become decidedly less political as well as less partisan. This de-politicization shows itself in the election of leaders and the foci of activity.

Leadership tickets within unions used to be organized according to political party affiliation; this was particularly the case under the years of Allende, and in the early 1980s under Pinochet when the unions first started to resume organizing. Leadership according to partisanship is no longer the norm amongst most Chilean unions. Even within the CUT, Chile's largest and most politically active labor confederation, it is currently up for debate whether or not they will continue electing the executive committee and advisory council on a partisan ticket. Argues Manuel Bustos, CUT's president, "we may politick among ourselves, but politics is out there not here (in unions). We have to fight for other things now."[15] The federation of public employees (ANEP) has already ceased to elect its leaders by party list.

Since the transition to democracy, several of labor's strategies, objectives and relations with political parties have changed. According to labor expert Patricio Frías (1993: 52), during the period 1980–1988, the overriding union strategy in Chile was that of strikes and marches coordinated with political parties and social movements meant to destabilize the military regime, with the objective of returning to democracy. Although many of the strategies remain the same, the political goals have fallen by the wayside for unions. "We concern ourselves with the worker and workplace now. The only politics is that which goes on inside the unions and there is too much. Do we march still? We march, we strike, but now because of wages — they are minimal, and because of health care and insurance."[16] Other goals, less political and more specifically related to the workplace, have replaced the unions' objective of toppling the dictatorship. Bustos also adds that their relationship with the political parties has changed, becoming "more

autonomous" and "less involved in everyday life (of the confederation)."[17] However, of all organizations within civil society, it appears
to be the unions which are most active in the formulation and lobbying of government legislation. The CUT has participated in various tri-lateral meetings with the Minister of the Treasury or
Minister of Economy and legislators. For example in April of 1991,
the leaders of the CUT met with Alejandro Foxley (Minister of the
Treasury), President Aylwin, and other union leaders to discuss new
legislation on minimum wage and pensions. Although the level of
politicization of unions has markedly decreased since then, labor
still keeps one hand in the political process.[18]

Among the few feminist (identity) organizations that continue to
exist following the transition back to democracy, there has also
been a marked shift from issues and activities that deal with political democracy or government policies to more social themes.[19]
Testimony of this process of de-politicization among identity
organizations comes from both anecdotal evidence, as well as from
the study of the yearly commemoration of International Women's
Day. According to one of the long-time directors of *Tierra Nuestra*
(the umbrella organization for women's identity groups in the
southern zone of Santiago) their organizations used to spend
approximately 80 percent of their time and efforts on anti-authoritarian projects: denouncing human rights abuses, searching for
disappeared family members, campaigning for a democratic
regime, lobbying for laws to protect women's rights, teaching
women about their role as participants under the emerging democracy. These groups now report expending less than a quarter of
their energies on such issues, almost all of which is devoted to the
role of women as voters and participants in democracy. The other
75 percent of their time and resources is instead spent on cultural
events celebrating women's identity and achievements, seminars
on domestic abuse or household finances, or self-improvement
courses based on the empowerment of women.[20]

Perhaps most illustrative of the de-politicization of women's
identity groups is the transformation over time of the chants and
convocatorios (calls to assemble issued by a coalition of women's
identity groups) of the March 8 (International Women's Day) com-
memorations, which were usually in the form of a march followed

by a cultural presentation. In 1977, women were called to the commemoration to "relate the history of the feminist movement, to underscore the harshness of the military regime and the anguish of the mothers, wives, relatives of the disappeared, political prisoners."[21] Similarly, International Women's Day celebrations throughout the late 1970s and 1980s included a cultural and artistic event, as well as a "great political-*revindicativo* content." Commemoration participants typically joined together in chants such as: "For democracy and life, we fight united" (1987), "Women, united, to reconstruct democracy" (1988), and "Democracy works because women are present" (1989). As tensions heightened over the desired means of governance, the *convocatorios* to these marches also became increasingly political, linking women's equality with political (democratic) equality:

> March 1986: *Let's take a new step, uniting our hands with the women of the world. Every new step brings us closer to conquering spaces of freedom in our conscience and action, in our organizations and in our Homeland. We believe that it is only from the sum of the libertarian and democratic consciences that a new Chile will be born, leaving behind the nightmare of authoritarianism and intolerance with its memory of death, misery and pain. We invite you to take this new step on International Women's Day in order to express, united, the firm decision to begin the great offensive against the dictatorship.*

> March 1987: *Chilean women,... we call you to unite with us and act for the following things: respect for our lives and development with access to resources of nutrition, health, education, housing, recreation. Elimination of all forms of discrimination against women in the judicial, labor and cultural realms. Participation of women in all levels of decision-making. An end to repression, to torture, to death and to exile. An end to the dictatorship and all authoritarianism. The conquest of our full rights as women goes hand in hand with our liberation as a people. On International Women's Day, let's return to lift our voices in solidarity!*

Similar *convocatorios* were issued for the marches in 1988, 1989, and 1990.

However, both the tone and the content changed in 1991 following the transition of power from an authoritarian to a democratic government. The majority of the chants of the Santiago march and celebration were of the following vein: "I am human, I am equal, I am free" and "We won once, we will win again." The *convocatorio* for International Women's Day 1991 in Chile began with a review of the efforts and advances women made in ending the dictatorship and repression. The actual call to assemble was decidedly less political than in previous years, focusing more upon the solidarity of women:

> Woman, if you have the desire to be with other women, to show your strength, to share your creativity, pain, successes, loneliness, happiness, fears and hopes, we invite you to unite your voice with ours and organized we will break the silence that has characterized our dark and hidden history.... this is an opportunity to make International Women's Day recognized not only by a part of Chilean society, but by all its sectors. We want to make our country understand that the eighth of March is for the woman what the first of May is for the worker. Organized women, let's debate about various proposals and bring together our goals. You will be the protagonist.

In the most recent years, since the 1992 push towards the decentralization of government, March 8 has largely been celebrated on the municipal level, with chants for "Equality for women, abuse for no one" and "Women, united, will never be divided." Women's identity organizations have begun to put the period of military rule behind them (although never forgotten, they will tell you), and focus on issues of women's rights, domestic abuse, and capacitation and formation of women.

In the area of women's legal rights, Chilean law (as is true in many other Latin American countries) contains several provisions which encroach upon women's sexuality and choice, including their right to an abortion or divorce. And until the early 1990s, physical domestic abuse was not unlawful. With the end of authoritarian rule, women are free to pursue other political challenges. So why do women's identity groups not expend more time and effort on lobbying for changes in government policies? There are two major reasons. First, the Catholic Church continues to be a strong force throughout Latin America, and it also continues its ardent opposition to abortion, birth control and divorce. Any of these issues around which women mobilized would be blocked by the Catholic Church; an example of this occurred in July of 1994, when the Archbishop called on women not to seek a divorce law.[22] Since the ties are so strong between many of the Latin American governments and the Church, a government would rarely be willing to risk that relationship by sanctioning activities which are against the wishes of the Church. As one Chilean woman explained to me, "the government and the church are in bed together in order to prevent more sins...but I didn't even know that they were married."

The second reason that identity groups are not more active in the formulation of Chilean policies was discussed in the previous chapter — that women and their issues have become institutionalized under the state structure. Since the inception of the National Service for Women (*Servicio Nacional de la Mujer*, SERNAM), a cabinet-level ministry whose director is appointed by the president, the government has encouraged all demands related to women's issues to be channeled through SERNAM. As an arm of the state, SERNAM is thus unlikely to propose legislation that will not be condoned by the government — much of the feminist agenda falls under this category. With the most effective policy route closed to the feminist agenda, identity groups have withdrawn from the legislative and policy arenas, and many have suffered significant losses in membership and funding.[23]

The de-politicization issue is less black-and-white for territorial organizations, of which our case studies continue to be the neighborhood associations (*Juntas de Vecinos*) and the mothers' centers (*Centros de Madres*, CEMAs). On the whole in civil society, territorial organizations became politicized in the 1980s to a much lesser extent than functional or identity groups; in fact, the former often did not increase their level of politicization during the authoritarian regime. Political activities were almost non-existent among neighborhood councils and CEMAs under the Pinochet years; however, it was not at all uncommon for an organization to claim an affiliation (publicly or not) with a particular party or ideology.[24]

In the decade preceding military rule, the ideology and activities of the neighborhood associations were politicized. In the late 1960s, these councils were looked on as political organizations in the sense that they served as "*una voz convocatoria*," a space through which the people presented their demands to both the local and national governments within Frei's program of "*Promoción Popular.*"[25] Under Allende, the neighborhood councils were also very strong and active; they were a space for the representation of local interests and in some communities were highly militarized by political parties; many councils actively espoused a political ideology. With the advent of authoritarian rule, the Pinochet government left the neighborhood associations relatively untouched compared to other organizations. Although the *Diario Oficial* law #349 (March 13, 1974) gave the government the right to ask for the resignation of any organization leader at any time, the law was rarely applied to the councils except in the cases of some leftist neighborhoods.[26]

Notwithstanding, the *Juntas* swiftly lost their facility to represent interests because the military government closed almost all channels of citizen participation. Their inability to represent local interests and the fact that leaders within the neighborhood councils came to be appointed instead of voted upon, led to a de-legitimation and de-politicization of these organizations. Explains an ex-member of a council, "I stopped participating in the early 1980s, there around 1982, because we (our *Junta*) were just going in circles (*dando vuelta*) in the *barrio*."[27] Under Pinochet, the councils began to focus almost exclusively upon small neighborhood projects, forfeiting (or being denied) their previous role as a channel of representation between the people and the national and local governments. The once-frequent meetings with government bureaucrats and the municipality's mayor fell by the wayside, as neighborhood councils instead began to direct their energies to self-help solutions about street conditions, neighborhood lighting, garbage collection, block parties, and children's projects.

Although among councils political activity was almost non-existent during the military regime, political ideology maintained a strong presence. Usually this occurred because all the elected or appointed leaders of a particular council hailed from the same political party, or were all pro- or anti-government. Even though this common ideology rarely translated itself into action, it discouraged (sometimes actively) the participation of non-politically aligned members in the councils. Following the transition to democracy, many councils surrendered even this small vestige of the political realm. The following two case studies help illustrate the rise and decline of the politicization of the neighborhood associations.

The *comuna* of Providencia is an upper-middle class neighborhood, encompassing chic clothing boutiques, prim cafes, and a scattering of the older, more established residential streets in Santiago. It has long-served as a home to conservative forces; and it is only in the most recent decade with the transition to neo-liberal economics and the birth of the nouveau-riche class that it has lost its stature of highest prestige to zones of newer, monolithic construction closer to the mountains. Throughout the 1980s, a neighborhood association of Providencia[28] had three main projects: planning social events for adults, helping families in economic hardship, and "neighborhood vigilance." In an interview with a council member, it was revealed that the latter meant being on the lookout for "that which might cause damage to our neighborhood, our neighbors, or *mi General*."[29] Yet Pinochet did not live in Providencia. This was not good-neighborliness — it was a project of patriotism, whose intent was to ferret out opposition supporters and turn them in to the government. Since the transition to democracy, the vigilance program has left political partisanship on the side to focus instead on preventing street crime and discouraging graffiti artists in the neighborhood.

On the other hand, the *comuna* of Pedro Aguirre Cerda is a low-income neighborhood with half of its streets still unpaved, problems with its water and refuse systems, and high levels of unemployment. Residents are largely, although not entirely, of the political left. Pedro Rodríguez, who left his post in 1992 after serving for twenty years as the president of the neighborhood association, recounts that there has occurred a marked, yet unmeasurable, change in the council; although their budgetary allocations have not changed, nor have their activities, the *"onda"* (atmosphere) of the council is distinct. Political tensions have subsided. During the 1980s, almost all of the members and leaders of the neighborhood association belonged to the Socialist Party (PS) or the leftist Party for Democracy (PPD). Rodríguez reports that nearly one-third of their current membership is comprised of those who have joined since 1990; and although no official census is taken within the council, he estimates that nearly all of the new members pertain to other political parties, mostly the Christian Democratic Party (PDC) or the National Renovation Party (RN), or refrain completely from political participation. Unfortunately, although most councils keep minutes of their meetings, such documentation is usually discarded every few years, or when a new president is elected.[30] Rodríguez recalls how the tone of the meetings changed after the democratic government came to power:

> Before (democracy), we went here and there working in the community but always with a blanket of politics hanging over us, over everything. We, as a group (the Junta), never entered into the political, but political sayings always entered into the meetings. We would complain that the streets were not paved and that when the rains came everything would flood. Well, someone would say that Pinocchio (nickname for Pinochet) wanted us to flood so that he would have an excuse to organize a real navy...we all always laughed at these jokes because we were all from the same color (political side)...Well, now that part of our meetings left, it just left, now we only complain, that's it. No, sometimes we throw blame but we could throw it on anyone, on the capitalists, on the banks, on the concejales (municipal representatives), on the government.[31]

Even though this change in tone is not measurable, it is clearly something that is present in the minds of the actors. The political innuendoes have subsided in the meetings. There are thus cases in which the activities of the neighborhood associations have become less political (as in the Providencia case study), and other instances in which it is merely the overtones of the organization which have changed (the council in Pedro Aguirre Cerda).

On the other hand, the goal of the mothers' centers (*Centros de Madres*, CEMAs) was to de-politicize women by directing their energies and time into a neighborhood organization where they would receive training in artisan skills and lessons on how to be a better wife and mother. As one of the national directors of CEMA-Chile explains, "we (the volunteers) had nothing to do with politics; we helped them (the women) get their houses, take care of their children and taught them hygiene, interpersonal relations, and about habits."[32] Directed by Pinochet's wife Lucía Hiriat, the CEMAs were re-designed under the dictatorship to channel women into traditional roles which were then defined as non-political roles. It was thought that by pigeon-holing women into their homes as mothers and wives, and by providing them with "invaluable" training, they would support the military government — because of gratitude for the skills learned, and because of a perceived inability to break out of traditional home-bound roles and participate in the political realm. Therefore, the act of de-politicizing women became, in effect, a political act. Although the goals and activities of the CEMAs were decidedly non-political, their symbolism or reputation for reinforcing authoritarian rule and women's support of it may be considered to be political.

After the return to democracy in Chile, the CEMAs retained their reputation for social conservatism, but the perceived political implications of their support of women's traditional roles seemed to decrease. It is not that the CEMAs de-politicized — they were never really political organizations; it is just that the political implications of their actions lessened. This may be attributed to two factors. First, unlike the dictatorship, the current democratic government has not taken the traditional stance that women should be in the home, therefore, CEMA could no longer be perceived as aligning with those in political power. Second, nearly one-half of CEMAs women volunteers (most of whom supported the military regime and hailed from the political right and the upper class) stopped participating in the organization after the transition to democracy; therefore, their influence to link CEMA to the political right greatly diminished.[33] Nevertheless, because Lucia Hiriat de Pinochet continued to be the director, CEMA still retained its right-wing, political symbolism.

On a side note, some may argue that organizations' activities and meetings are not necessarily the best measure of the level of de-politicization of civil society. Instead, they might suggest that if funding and grant applications are any indication, citizens' organizations continue to be political entities.[34] However, many of the organization leaders I interviewed noted that what they write in their proposals is based upon what they believe the donor wants to hear. In other words, they are instrumental or rational actors in their approach. If they perceive that the donor wishes to fund projects related to consolidating democracy, they will couch their project in similar terms in order to "sell it." There is no indication that such applications would be an accurate measure of an organization's level of politicization. Demonstrating an awareness of politics and its import through a funding application, and participating politically in society, are not the same beast.

Groups may claim political motives or actions in their grant proposals, but the above examination of what actually occurs within the organizations themselves demonstrates that organized participation becomes increasingly less political following a transition back to democracy. This is, of course, a general trend and thus exists to varying degrees within civil society as a whole and within each individual organization. Yet the question remains, why does this de-politicization occur?

WHY DOES ORGANIZATIONAL DE-POLITICIZATION OCCUR?

Citizens' groups do not become less political in a vacuum. Instead, a changing environment provides the parameters in which organizations must function and be flexible if they are to survive. In the case of (re)democratization, there are aspects and by-products of the transition which may cause organizations to de-politicize.

The Achievement Of Goals

All organizations have one or more goals — they are their *raisons d'être*. Organizations are not founded merely for the sake of existing, but for coalescing a common identity, solving a problem, accomplishing a project, affecting a change, or acquiring benefits or goods. As goals are achieved, the organization either replaces them with new goals, or disbands. Chapter 3 proved that most organizations do not disappear after a transition to democracy, instead they transform. The phenomenon of de-politicization indicates that instead of being committed to political participation in general, these organizations were most interested in the achievement of just (one) specific political goal(s). Therefore, as groups achieve their political goal(s), they may branch out into other realms. For many organizations, the actual transition away from authoritarian rule signifies the achievement or end of their political goal(s).

For example, the *Talleres Renacer* were founded because of economic reasons (high unemployment), but quickly became a form of political expression in the early 1980s. They began to make *arpilleras* as a source of extra income, but when their brothers, husbands and sons began to disappear, they chose to use their *arpilleras* as a form of political expression protesting human rights abuses of the dictatorship. As a result of their political actions, the *arpilleras* had to be made clandestinely, or they would be confiscated and the women, jailed. The women rationalized that since it was the military government that was taking away their male family members and therefore their income, one of their goals should be to get rid of Pinochet. With the return to democracy, the organizations have stopped their political activities and are now focusing on the social and economic realms. Whereas the *Talleres Renacer* used to count with numerous committees such as the Committee on Protests and Marches, the strongest and one of the only committees it has left is the *Comité de Comercio*; all of their political committees have been disbanded. The most significant reason for this organizational restructuring is that Pinochet is gone. In the words of one of their members, "*La política nuestra fue sacar a Pinochet. Cuando se acabó él, se acabó nuestra política.*"[35] With their only political goal resolved, the organizations are free to focus on other realms. The additional reasons — funding flight and disillusionment — are discussed below.

Part of the achievement of goals is that political conditions, namely the repression and lack of freedom, have objectively improved. This means that the need for political participation may be less, or at least less urgent; citizens may feel that they are finally able to focus on issues and activities which for years they have neglected because their energies were focused on supporting or defeating the military regime.

Disillusionment With Democracy

There are many politicians and academics who claim that an apathy falls over the general populace after a transition to democracy.

This is known as the "*desencanto*," the disenchantment with democracy. Yet it is important to be precise that what really occurs is: there is a *desencanto with politics*, not with participation as such.[36] To this end, the leader of the non-governmental organization CARITAS-Chile argues that the Aylwin government was merely administrating the transition but not promoting new policies due to a fear of Pinochet.[37] He therefore suggests that it is government policymaking that is absent, not citizen participation; hence, the "*desencanto*" is in response to the former, not the latter issue. As shown by the figures in Chapter 3, citizens are clearly still participating in civil society, although their efforts are now outside of the political realm.

Part of the disillusionment with democracy is that following the transition, the political arena is often more closed, competitive or corrupt than citizens expected.[38] Most of the subjects interviewed for this study said that they thought that government decision-making would be more open to participation by citizens. Explains a neighborhood association leader, "when we sang '*Gana, la gente, Aylwin presidente*' I thought that meant that we were all being elected. Now we can't even enter the presidential palace or the municipality."[39] Before the transition organizations were very political in nature; it was in the streets and in the homes that plans were made to topple the dictatorship. Now, politics often centers around the "closed doors" of the municipality and elected offices. Much of the local decision-making and political strength centers around the *concejales* (which are elected and from among which the mayor is elected). The *concejales* are now the official via of the political parties, thereby leaving citizens' organizations out of the "political loop."[40] Due to such changes in the participatory process, people have become disillusioned with political democracy:

> If you bring in (si se meta) the politics of political parties, everything goes out the window (se echa a perder las cosas) like in the years of Allende. The only thing we (unions) have achieved politically was the exit of Pinochet, and that was without political parties. Politics is dirty, especially within political parties. It is only about self-interest.[41]

Democracy didn't arrive, happiness didn't come.[42]

*We, the poor people, are so screwed by democracy — how much they
promised us, but nothing! They haven't even given us so much as a piece of
candy.*[43]

Following the transition back to democracy, citizens seem to
become disillusioned with democracy as well as with those who
implement democratic procedures beyond the local level.
The first quotation above reflects not only the disillusionment
with democracy, but also the legacy of distrust of political parties
among the populace. There exists a widespread fear that too much
participation in the political system might lead Chile's democracy
to re-visit the problems it experienced under the Allende years.
Therefore, some believe that although it is acceptable and even
necessary to participate in civil society, one must tread lightly in
the realm of politics. Also, after a long-fought battle against a dictator or in favor of democracy, politically active citizens are often
tired, cautious or disillusioned with politics. Whether the outcome
was not as they had expected or they just need a respite from the
same old issues, it is difficult to continue to mobilize citizens
around political matters. Other issues take the fore, particularly
economics.

The Economics Of Participation

There are two economic factors which adversely affect the level of
politicization of organizations. First, a transition to democracy
often serves as a red light for international funding to groups of
civil society. Such a transition initially brings a wealth of support
for the bolstering of state institutions, the training of state employees, and the re-structuring of military and police forces. Countries
such as those of Eastern Europe which experience a simultaneous
transition of their economic system also benefit from significant
international aid in that realm. Yet much of the international non-
governmental funding, or "solidarity" support, for civil society has
exited Latin American countries on the heels of their transitions.
For example, the *Talleres Renacer* used to receive more than sufficient

funds for their numerous projects, nearly 70% of which came from an undisclosed non-governmental organization in Denmark. With the transition to democracy, the Danish NGO withdrew the funding, purportedly to send it to another country that was struggling in the pre-transition stage of democratization. While making their exit from Chile, the Danish NGO even asked the *Talleres Renacer* if they would like to contribute to their new project!

Organizations are also vulnerable to changes in domestic funding following a transition back to democracy. Since the priorities of the regimes are distinct, their funding patterns will reflect these differences. For example, state funding of the mothers' centers was cut nearly in half after the transfer to democratic power, reflecting the strong connection between the CEMAS and the dictatorship. It is in fact the economic aspect of politics itself that drives many organizations to de-politicize:

> *Before the transition, we (citizens' organizations) were rewarded and admired for pushing the limits of politics, rewarded by NGOs and foreign governments. Now, we must be careful of what we say or we won't receive funding or support. If we support the government, we receive no funding because it is nothing new. If we suggest alternatives, we receive no funding because it is not in line with the democratic government. So we just don't do politics.*[44]

Many organizations, spanning the political spectrum, report similar patterns of funding flight or restrictions which significantly depress political organizing. With such a decrease in the available funds and resources, groups must become more self-sufficient if they are to survive. In this case, the means often become the ends. As groups begin to collect membership dues, make small investments, and produce goods or offer services for sale, their members become increasingly aware and interested in economic issues.

The third factor which leads to the "economization" of organizations is that many of those in the lower income brackets have still not reaped the benefits of neo-liberal reform. In Chile, widely known for its "economic miracle," approximately 38 percent of the population lives under the poverty line, an improvement of four percentage points over 1990 levels.[45] Some citizens choose to transform their organizations into part-time "micro-enterprises," in which they divide the profits from their sales between the organization itself and the participating members. Although the impact of such programs is likely to be negligible on the national economy, families and small communities do notice the benefits. UNICEF also acknowledges possible gains from such participation, arguing that the organizations of civil society "constitute a promise and a hope of an unexploited fountain of new resources to confront the economic situation" (UNICEF et al, 1993: 141). It is largely the functional sustenance organizations and the cultural territorial groups that adopt this self-help posture, leading them even further from the political realm.

The OEPs provide a helpful illustration of this process of "economization" of organizations; since 1990, the activities of popular economic organizations have taken on a much greater economic component.[46] Up until then, most of the OEP funding came from the non-governmental organization NOVIB through the Catholic Church's *Vicaría de Solidaridad*.[47] From 1991–1993, the Vicaría underwent a series of transformations to become, instead, two organizations focusing on religious work (the *Vicaría Pastoral-Social*) and youth issues (the *Vicaría de la Esperanza*). The OEPs fell in neither category, and in addition, the donations that used to trickle in from international organizations were rapidly disappearing. Faced with the prospect of little or no funding, another non-governmental organization PROSAN took over helping the OEPs in organizing themselves to become self-sufficient. This was a necessary step "since the resources have diminished, it is necessary to create initiatives to raise our own resources so that we can continue cooking together" (PROSAN, 1992: 5–6). Money from NOVIB and PROSAN continued during the early 1990s to "re-convert" the OEPs into micro-enterprises so that they, and their projects, would become self-sufficient. One *olla comun* (in San Antonio) had a bread baking project. But in order to expand that project beyond their neighborhood, they needed a semi-industrial oven; PROSAN gave them a three-year loan in order to purchase the oven. In La Pincoya, a group of *ollas* took over the preparation and sale of school lunches to primary school children in one school; it was a way for them to earn money for the *olla*, and to provide a community service. Other *ollas comunes* in Pudahuel raise money through bread or pastry sales, using much of the earnings to give free milk to students.

OEPs are now also branching out into new activities beyond local soup kitchens and craft workshops. For example, since September of 1990, there has been a joint milk project with FOSIS (the government's Fund for Solidarity and Social Investment), in which the women of the *ollas* comunes do community service by providing cereal and milk to children and senior citizens. Others have begun to sell their wares beyond the boundaries of their communities — at stores in Santiago, or on the international market. As one member of an OEP stated, "Starting a (new) project is the more or less easiest way to achieve the objective that the *ollas* continue functioning in the future. To start a project means the following: create workshops, for example, bread bakeries, childcare centers, so that we don't lose the organization that has taken us so many years to build".[48] Oxhorn gives an account of an OEP created in 1975, which was a productive workshop specializing in *arpilleras*. In 1991, the workshop also lost all of its funding and meeting space from the Vicaría. Within a few months, the workshop had located new work-space and was operating at least as successfully as before (Oxhorn, 1992: 430fn). Many such workshops are now also producing blankets or sweaters for domestic and international sale, as well as holding workshops on accounting and finance. Faced with these economic priorities and pressures, political activities have fallen by the wayside.

It is important to note that such measures towards self-sufficiency are more prevalent among functional and identity organizations; they are the groups most susceptible to fluctuations in funding because of their dependence upon NGO donations. Territorial organizations rely almost entirely upon municipal or state funds and membership dues, which oscillate with less frequency.

Yet all types of organizations show this trend towards de-politicization. Achievement of their goal(s), disillusionment with democracy, and the financial realities of participation lead to a decidedly economic focus among organizations. After a transition, neither democracy nor its institutions or implementors are the targets of democratic participation. The advent of a long-awaited democratic regime seems to be a signal to citizens that they can now focus on other issues. Civil society may embrace democratic participation, but it shuns — and is discouraged from — political participation. As we will see in the next chapter, many organizations couple de-politicization with other transformational strategies to adapt to the new democratic regime.

Notes

1. An idiomatic phrase commonly heard in Chile (a *"chilenismo"*), roughly meaning "I'm not into politics."

2. Slogan of organized mine workers in Chuquicamata (northern Chile); as cited in Petras and Leiva (1994: 161).

3. As told by Winnie Lira, Director of the Fundación Solidaridad, in an interview with the author, July 15, 1994; later confirmed with women participants in the *taller*.

4. Points one through four below represent a synthesis of the arguments of Alvarez, 1990 (point 3); Huntington, 1968 (point 2); Pateman, 1989 (points 2, 3, 4); Razeto et al, 1990 (point 1); and Rousseau, 1762 (points 2, 3, 4). See Chapter 1 for a greater elaboration of the debate concerning the role of participation under democracy. These points were also discussed extensively in author's interview with Cecilia Aguayo, Director of the Division of Community Development of the Municipality of San Joaquín, August 24, 1994; and also in author's interview with Lira, op.cit.

5. See Marysa Navarro's "The Personal is Political: Las Madres de la Plaza de Mayo" in Eckstein (ed.), 1989, pp. 241–258 for an application of this idea to Latin America. This position is also furthered by Chilean feminist Julieta Kirkwood who posits that authoritarianism and patriarchy are two forms of political dominance, one in the traditional sense and one in the non-traditional sense, but both must be eradicated before a free democracy is possible (Kirkwood, 1981 and 1982). See also Lourdes Arizpe's forward in Jelin (1990), and essays in the collection by Held (1987).

6. This assertion was made by many of those interviewed, most notably: Raúl Rettig, President of the Commission on Truth and

Reconciliation, author's interview, August 11, 1992; and Cristián Precht, Vicar General and first Vicar of the Vicaria de la Solidaridad, author's interview, September 25, 1992.

7.   See footnote 3, chapter 3 for details on the margin of error and sampling problems of this data. Source: *"Compendio Estadísticos,"* National Institute of Statistics, Santiago, Chile.

8.   These statistics are for all of Chile; the corresponding growth rates for the Metropolitan Region of Santiago are, respectively, 349% and -31%. While almost all functional, non-political organizations dramatically increased their total numbers within Chile between 1988 and 1992, many experienced a slight decrease in numbers within the Metropolitan region. These statistics, and those of the following sentence, represent the author's calculations based on data from the *"Compendio Estadísticos,"* op. cit.

9.   As reported in *La Segunda*, August 2, 1991; survey completed by CEP-Adimark.

10.   *Centros de Estudios Públicos*, December 1993, pp. 20, 53–57; and December 1989, p. 34 and appendix; and articles in *El Mercurio*.

11.   As noted in interview with Lira, op cit.

12.   Maria Paz Ortega O., Secretary of Supplies of a *huerto* (a communal planting group) in the *comuna* of Puente Alto, in interview with the author on September 1, 1994.

13.   As recounted to me by four members of Talleres Genesis, three of whom wish to remain anonymous; the fourth member identified herself as Maria Angelica. They requested anonymity because the organization was supposed to be a non-political entity, and they were instructed not to discuss their political activities. Interviews with the author in Santiago, July 1992 and July 1994.

14.   In interview with the author on August 3, 1994, Santiago.

15.   Manuel Bustos, in interview with the author on July 29, 1994.

16.   Abelino Quilaqueo Peralta, Treasurer of the Sindicato de Trabajadores Cecinas Super, in interview with the author on August 10, 1994, Santiago.

17.   Bustos, op. cit. He was, however, unable or unwilling to provide more specific examples of this change in relationship of unions and political parties.

18.   The "neo-politicization" of the unions in the 1980s was also noted by theorist Alain Touraine, who observed that it was the country itself that

became the central object of labor's demands (cited in Barrera and Falabella, 1989: 240).

19.   As discussed in Chapter 6, the universe of feminist (identity) organizations since the transition to democracy is a very small N, since many of these groups have ceased to exist.

20.   These percentages are estimates as related by Rosita Esquinolas, co-director of Tierra Nuestra, in interview with the author on August 25, 1994. Recall the above discussion that although many, including myself, consider these activities to be loaded with political content, they are decidedly non-political in this study's narrower confines of "the political" as relating to government policies, state institutions, or regime type.

21.   This quotation, and all the ensuing quotations on the next two pages with respect to women's marches, were taken from Gaviola, 1994; as well as the author's own observation of the marches in March 1989, 1990, and 1992.

22.   It is important to note that the Chilean divorce law is unique in Latin America.

23.   See Chapter 6 for a more in-depth and comprehensive discussion of this phenomenon, as well as for concrete examples.

24.   Unlike with functional and identity groups, there are no measurable factors to indicate the level of politicization of territorial organizations; therefore, the conclusions drawn in the section are from an in-depth study of two Juntas — one in a right-wing, upper-middle class neighborhood and the other in a predominantly leftist, lower-income neighborhood.

25.   For more detailed information about Frei's program, and about participation prior to authoritarian rule in Chile, see Chapter 2.

26.   For example, this occurred in the *comunas* of La Bandera and Pudahuel.

27.   Elena Godoy de Rodríguez, former Junta member in Pedro Aguirre Cerda and wife of the council's President (at the time of her departure), in interview with the author on August 12, 1994.

28.   Bounded by Avenida Providencia, Manuel Montt and Pedro de Valdívia.

29.   The information and quotations concerning this Junta in Providencia come from anonymous interviews with two members, one of which was a leader of the association, and with Isidoro Leal, President of

the *Junta* from 1990 to 1994; interviews with the author in August 1992 and 1994.

30.   This information regarding the *Junta* in Pedro Aguirre Cerda is taken from two interviews with Rodríguez (July 1992 and August 1994), with Godoy de Rodríguez (August 1992), and is corroborated through various conversations with members of the *Junta* in July of 1992.

31.   Rodríguez, interview with the author on August 29, 1994.

32.   Bertita Benavente, past-national director of the *Voluntariado* and regional vice-president of CEMA, in interview with the author on August 17, 1994.

33.   Benavente, interview, op. cit. Benavente counts herself among those who no longer participate in CEMA or its sister-organizations: the *Centros Abiertos* for children or the *Voluntariado* (volunteer pool). Through 1996, Lucia Hiriat de Pinochet continued to be the director of CEMA-Chile.

34.   This approach was brought to my attention by Michael Shifter of the Ford Foundation in Santiago, Chile in a conversation in July 1992. Organizations that are not self-sufficient may request funding from government agencies, non-governmental organizations, and especially in cases of decentralization, the municipality.

35.   Maria Nuñez, coordinator of the Talleres Renacer, in interview with the author on August 10, 1994. Translated, it means, "Our politics was to get rid of Pinochet. When he left, our politics left."

36.   As pointed out to me by James March, the other problem of claiming "disenchantment" is that there are complications of distinguishing disenchantment from the articulation of conflicting interests among the citizenry.

37.   As argued by Christián Vives, Director of CARITAS Chile, in interview with the author on September 6, 1992. Rodolfo Larrea, a student leader of the FECH, used a different argument to discredit the existence of apathy amongst the Chilean populace. In an interview with the author he claimed that cries of "apathy" and *"desencanto"* are "the scapegoat some (state) leaders use to explain why people are not participating in their project or organization." August 1, 1992.

38.   Given the high expectations citizens living under a repressive regime often have of democracy, it is inevitable that many are disappointed with the resulting product. In the case of Chile, *"para los sectores marginados por la omnipresencia del poder autoritario, la democracia llegó a ser la expresión de la maximización de lo plural, de lo hetergeneo, de lo descentrado, lugar de la diferencias*

que ... *otorgaría espacio político y discursivo a toda minoría... 18 anos de supresiones proyectaron, en el imaginario social la idea de democracia como el escenario de una ficción posible, como el lugar de inter-cambio conel imposible que se vivía"* (Olea, 1992: 30).

39.   Pedro Rodriguez, op. cit.

40.   Examples of where such a political structure occurs are in the *comunas* of San Joaquin and Pudahuel in Santiago, Chile.

41.   Jose Ortega, General Secretary of the *Sindicato de Hipodromo* Chile, in interview with the author, August 16, 1994.

42.   In reference to the opposition's slogan during the 1988 plebiscite which claimed "*Chile, la alegría ya viene...*". Tina, member of a workshop in *Talleres Genesis*, in an interview with the author on August 3, 1994.

43.   Silvia, president of an OEP workshop, in interview with the author on July 20, 1994.

44.   Verónica Mátus, chair of the women's department of the Chilean Human Rights Commission, interview with the author, August 9, 1994. Ms. Mátus was also highly involved in women's identity organizations throughout the 1980s.

45.   See Frías, 1992: 5, and Petras et al, 1994.

46.   For an argument that women never saw their participation in OEPs as political, see T. Rio Caldeira in Jelin, 1990: 57–61.

47.   Author's interview with Mejia, op. cit.

48.   OEP member as quoted in PROSAN, 1992: 7–8.

CHAPTER FIVE

Organizational Transformation:

Recycling for the Environment

> You (gringos) worry about the
> environment, and we do too. You
> recycle, we recycle. Here in
> Pudahuel, we recycle organizations
> — we use what was there to make
> something new.[1]

> We are now just organizations
> mirándose al umbligo.[2]

A previous chapter established that with the notable exception of
women's identity (feminist) groups, most organizations outlive a
transition back to democracy. How they do so — by recycling
themselves or merely mirándose al umbligo — is what is now in question. If organizations do not de-mobilize following re-democratization, where and how do they continue to exist? The applicable
hypothesis, as presented in the first chapter, is that organizations
are reactive and flexible entities. Faced with a change in their environment, they will choose to adapt and survive to avoid death (disbanding); I have referred to this strategy as the path of transformation. One aspect of this path, as covered in Chapter 4, is that
organizations persist by moving away from the (traditional) political realm. They also transform by becoming *more localized (changing
the level of organizing), more particularistic (changing target), and at times, by
widening the scope of their activities (changing domain).* In order to outlive
re-democratization, organizations need not adopt all four "tactics."
Just one transformational tactic may be sufficient to allow a group
to weather the uncertainty and turbulence of a dramatic change in
its political environment.

115

Transitions back to democracy introduce several far-reaching changes to the political system which affect the opportunities for citizens' participation. For example, there may be less room for small organizations in the electoral realm as political parties re-emerge. In other words, there may now exist too much competition for resources and contacts for social organizations and political parties to function in the same arenas. The end of dictatorship also may signal the end of a national issue which was urgent and broad enough to unite the far-reaching interests of civil society; with a move away from authoritarian rule, it may be nearly impossible to find a single issue around which so many citizens and groups are again willing to cooperate. All of these changes occurred in Chile following the transition back to democracy; and as a consequence, organizations have become atomized. In Chile, re-democratization was also an indication that citizens no longer "needed" to focus on the regime type, and could once again focus their attention and energies on their personal needs. Lastly, state power (largely the responsibility for finances and administration) has been de-centralized to the Chilean municipalities; most organizations have therefore transferred their focus to the municipal level as well.

A few caveats are necessary as an introduction to this chapter. First, as one might imagine, these different facets of transformation are often interrelated. In some cases, they cannot be disaggregated in order to fit nicely into just one defined category of organizational transformation. Take, for example, a small organization which used to have as its core the protest of human rights abuses of the dictatorship. Now, following the transition back to democracy, the group instead provides classes for neighborhood women on child-rearing, personal development and household finances; it also runs a day-care center for the members' children. Is this to be classified as a transformation of the level, target, or domain of the organization? It is, of course, illustrative of all three types of transformation. Second, several of the cases depicted in the previous two chapters can also be seen as exemplary of the arguments herein. For example, the case of *Talleres Melipilla's* decision to end their participation in political rallies and election forums, and replace such activities with accounting or self-improvement workshops, could be classified as either de-politicization or particularism. This chapter should thus be read in tandem with Chapter 4. Finally, there is little measurable data available on these types of organizational transformation; therefore, this chapter relies heavily upon organizational histories gathered by the author from members and leaders of the relevant civil society groups. It is, consequently, the most anecdotal of the empirical chapters. Nevertheless, throughout all of my research in Latin America, I found not a single organization which had outlived re-democratization without employing at least one of these aspects of transformation. In this chapter, I address the three types of transformation separately, discussing how and why each manifests itself in the context of re-democratization.

Chapter 3 established that many groups persist after a transition back to democracy; however, they do not remain on the same trajectories. As one researcher argues, "one observes a process of greater articulation and, in some cases, redefinitions in the forms of functioning and in their activities that implies processes of greater development." OEPs (of food consumption) have not disappeared. "On the contrary, they remain and are going through an important process of redefinition" (Allan, 1991: 16, 29). In the cases of many organizations, this process of redefinition includes a localization of focus, a move to particularism, and an expansion of the domain of participation.

A LOCALIZATION OF CIVIL SOCIETY

Some organizations react to re-democratization by becoming more localized, a term which I use to include two types of transformation. First, groups move from focusing on state-level issues and organizing on a national level, to emphasizing neighborhood issues and participating in the municipal level. Non-territorial groups may also localize; they withdraw their organizational locus to that which is more immediate and directly related to their group. Second, civil society becomes atomized as social movements disintegrate; organizations begin to function as disconnected fragments, isolated from much horizontal contact with other organizations and political parties. Localization thus encompasses organizational transformation in the form of municipalization (neighborhood-focused) and fragmentation (lack of vertical ties). Logically, the phenomenon of localization occurs only among those groups which were not already localized; for example, *Juntas* will not undergo this process since their focus is already entirely on the local level. In fact, the official *Ley de Juntas de Vecinos* (#18.893) limits the neighborhood councils to the local level by not providing for provincial and national level federations; such umbrella groups were, however, permitted among *Juntas* under the prior democratic regime. Therefore, by definition and by law, the neighborhood councils operate on the local level. Fewer legal restraints are placed upon functional organizations; of such groups, those which localize do so for a variety of reasons.

First, during the years of the dictatorship when political parties were prohibited or severely constrained, civil society groups had a monopoly on organizing. Resources, potential members and space in which to mobilize were sufficient, and at times plentiful. Yet with re-democratization and the re-emergence of parties, some civil society groups chose (or were forced) to cede the national arena to political parties to avoid competition.[3] With the parties' focus on affecting policy and election outcomes, organizations are less likely to encounter such competition on the local level. In numerous interviews, participants also expressed the belief that their "occupation" of the national arena was merely that — their organizations were safeguarding that space until the parties re-emerged to claim it. Such an attitude clearly demonstrates the power of organizational and individual memory; there existed an expectation that societal groups would return to their positions and responsibilities of the prior democratic regime.

Second, a shift to the local level allows organizations to access new funds. Patterns of state funding of civil society groups have encouraged this trend towards localization. The new democratic government in Chile established FOSIS (Fund for Solidarity and Social Investment) in 1991 to provide financial support to civil society groups. The director reports that of the total number of proposals submitted, less than 20 percent are joint projects between two or more groups.[4] Most new projects are attempted on a small scale by a single organization; this is one indication that civil society is localized. The director also estimates that of the proposals accepted for funding, some eighty to ninety percent of them are local projects and FOSIS therefore suggests to them that they may also be eligible for funds from the municipality. The democratic government has greatly increased the funds and resources earmarked for municipal and regional development; the maturation and participation of civil society is considered to be part of such development. The government's budget for "de-centralized social programs" increased by 16.7% between 1990 and 1992.[5] After much of the international non-governmental funding left Chile for Eastern Europe in the early 1990s, social organizations are especially responsive to these new funding sources as a means of survival. As more funding becomes available for local projects, groups transfer their organizational focus to the local level.

There are also strong financial incentives on the municipal level for organizations to localize following the transition back to democracy. An advantage to working at the local level is that the municipalities often provide support to those groups which have *personalidad jurídica* (legal registration/recognition). The process of receiving this status can be difficult and discouraging, however such legal recognition allows organizations to sit on municipal advisory boards and gives them access to municipal resources, such as materials, meeting rooms and vehicles.

This funding pattern goes hand-in-hand with the third reason that groups localize: the process of de-centralization known as *municipalización*. Because this phenomenon contributes to multiple aspects of organizational transformation, and is often the driving force behind such changes, it is discussed below in a separate section.

Fourth, the end of the dictatorship left an organizational void in civil society. Under authoritarian rule, many groups and movements converged on the national level to fight the repressive political system. With democracy came the absence of a compelling national issue behind which to unite. The extreme heterogeneity of interests of the extant organizations meant that they were largely unable (or unwilling) to agree on a new common goal.[6] Not only could groups not agree on a common mission, they could not agree on the strategy with which they would approach a joint project. The change in political environment necessitated a change in organizational strategy if groups were to survive. Campero (1993) argues that the most challenging problem for organizations after a transition to democracy is how to move from a defensive and reactive strategy to an offensive pro-active one. Those that do not make this transition are usually those that are young and rigid (like women's identity groups), and they most often die. The organizations that remain become disconnected fragments within civil society; it is infinitely easier to unite groups in a defensive strategy against a common enemy that *is currently* injuring all of them than to get organizations and leaders to come to an agreement on a goal which *might in the future* be in their common interest. Groups are therefore more likely to fragment than to cooperate.

In what manner and to what extent has localization manifested itself? The following public opinion survey provides one indication of the degree to which organizations now favor the local level. The survey polled a random sample of Chilean organization leaders in fourteen *comunas* in 1993. The participants were provided with a list of positions, both governmental and non-governmental, local and national, and asked in whom their members had confidence to solve problems.[7] Topping the list of those in whom organization leaders had "no confidence" were political parties and provincial and national government, with 59.9% and 36.2% respectively. Those receiving the highest votes of "much confidence" were the municipality (41.3%) and the *Juntas de Vecinos* (37.4%). Citizens view the local level as the arena in which action translates to outcome, the arena in which their needs may be met.

During the height of civil society mobilization in the 1980s, the OEPs were highly "nationalized" organizations. Although their weekly activities focused on the local level (building houses, gardening, feeding the neighborhood), they also claimed a strong national component. The OEPs were connected to a vast network of social organizations which mobilized throughout the country around issues of human rights and poverty. They consistently interacted and cooperated with the Vicaría and the women's movement. Almost without exception, their focus is now overwhelmingly on the municipal level where they attempt to better the quality of life for the community and their families.[8]

OEPs have become localized in a two-fold manner. First, their principal contacts on the national level, namely the Vicaría and the women's movement, have dissipated. As noted in Chapters 4 and 6, most women's identity groups have virtually disappeared, rendering the women's movement immobile; and the Vicaría has undergone such a severe transformation that its new forms are hardly recognizable as vestiges of the prior organization. Now focusing entirely on pastoral and youth ministry, the Vicaría no longer acts as a magnet and organizing locus for national-level social movements. The Vicaría de Solidaridad (started as the Committee of Peace in 1973) is an organization linked to the Catholic Church. It helped people locate their loved ones, supported groups like OEPs, and attracted international attention to the human rights abuses of the Pinochet dictatorship. As the new democratic government assumed power, the Vicaría began to make plans to transform since its initial goals had been attained. As explained by Cristián Precht, the founding Vicar of the organization, the change was engineered by the leaders of the Vicaría. It was planned that the Vicaría of Solidarity would split into two organizations; the leaders, personnel, structure, and resources of the Vicaría would be passed on to these two groups. Beginning in late 1992, the Vicaría of Social Pastoral Work was created to minister to the needs of Catholics. At the same time, the Vicaría of Hope was started to focus on the needs of youths since almost 60 percent of the Chilean population is under 30. The first organization, in Precht's words, "represents a transformation of the Vicaría, the second organization is a case of mobilization. For the first, INDISO (a Catholic NGO) and the Vicaría will merge, change their structure and mission, united as a transformed organization" (interview with Precht, 1992). The two new Vicarías are thus more local in focus.

With the transformational changes in the Vicaría, the OEPs are left without a national movement with which to network and plan joint acts. There are even few vertical links within the universe of OEPs themselves. During the late 1980s, nearly every OEP belonged to an umbrella organization (or federation) which coordinated activities among themselves and with other civil society organizations, collected dues, published newsletters, and attracted international publicity and contacts. Now, many OEPs are withdrawing from their umbrella group because the dues were too expensive, and they didn't see that they received any tangible benefits from associating with the umbrella organization.[9] For those reasons, approximately 30% fewer umbrella groups exist today.[10] Forty percent of the OEPs I interviewed reported having no higher affiliation. OEPs now function largely as independent atoms.

Second, OEPs have localized by avoiding participating in debates, protests, and issues in the national arena since the transition back to democracy. The close of the dictatorship seems to have signaled to them that it was time to focus instead on local concerns which had long been neglected. I do not mean to imply that they entirely give up their original missions of feeding local families (*ollas comunes*), buying food in bulk at reduced rates (*comparando juntos*), or running a communal garden (*huertos*). These are localized activities which often remain intact in some similar form. It is the other half of their focus and activities which transforms. In many cases, the national focus of OEPs has been put aside in favor of a more local mission.

For example, in April of 1991, the *ollas comunes* of Pudahuel Norte held a series of meetings — first each *olla* met independently, and then they convened jointly — to discuss their future in terms of goals, projects, and structure.[11] They considered their financial situation, the status of the new government (meaning the democratic regime itself), and the extent of poverty in their communities. They made two decisions: 1) not to "take hold of anything we couldn't solve," and 2) to "leave politics to those in *Valpo*."[12] Led by the leaders of Pudahuel Norte, the OEP members voted to disband their respective "political" committees (i.e. Committee on Marches and Protests, Pro-Democracy and Social Development Committee). Individuals were encouraged to continue to participate in these activities, but the organizations would no longer sponsor such projects. Instead the members decided consensually to channel their energies into beginning a community service project. The OEP leaders decided to ask for project suggestions from the municipality. Doing so assured them that their project would fill a local need and would be likely to receive financial support from the municipality.[13] Their inquiries led them to a project for the elderly in which the OEPs of Pudahuel Norte opened a senior citizens' center where they provide breakfast and lunch daily, as well as offer workshops in knitting and gardening. Because it is a local project, funding is provided on a bi-annual basis by the municipality and the *Juntas*, supplemented by a one-time grant from FOSIS.[14] Other OEPs have localized by changing their focus to include youth centers, tree-planting campaigns, and school lunch programs; their connections to national campaigns, movements and issues have been replaced by a more local mission.

Unions have undergone a different process of localization. They have not become more focused on a local territory, rather their activities have become increasingly centered on issues immediate to their mission as workers. For example, the CUT's 1989 "Proposal for the Transition to Democracy," catapulted the confederation to a national level actor as it called on

> the future democratic government to resolve, in short order, the tremendous inequalities created by the Pinochet government...to this end, we re-claim an aggressive role for labor in the definition and initiation of the new politics which the transitional government must implement.

With the exception of demanding workers' autonomy, the document failed to address any topics specific to unions and unionists themselves. In stark contrast, the more recent (1993) "Proposal to the Presidential Candidates" was a document which focused almost entirely upon unions and workers themselves, largely ignoring the greater political context. The proposal demanded more latitude in collective negotiation, the right for all public employees to organize, an increase in the minimum wage, and more programs aimed at overcoming poverty. Now that the Chilean system has achieved the basic minimum in human rights and social development to make it "union-friendly," labor is less interested in trying to influence the greater political environment and more focused on the specific issues which will give unions increased power and independence within that environment. The locus of their activity has become more localized.

The Chilean labor movement has also experienced a great deal of fragmentation since the transition back to democracy. The labor movement has noticeably deteriorated; its contact and cooperation with other types of organizations, as well as between unions, have diminished.[15] While the CUT continues its stronghold on union organizing in Chile, there exists much discontentment within its ranks that the national organization is becoming estranged from the individual members and unions. The Secretary General of FETRASER gives as an example that his union has submitted several documents to the CUT's national directorship for revision; none of which has been responded to, nor returned. Hugo Arancibia of FEREPA concurs that their interactions with the CUT are *"bastante malas....*the CUT is very distant from its people."[16] Manuel Bustos, CUT's President, dismisses such allegations against the confederation, explaining that the fragmentation comes not from a distancing between the national and local leadership, but from a disagreement in the strategies and goals to be adopted.[17] He provides as an example the 1991 National Congress of the CUT which was marked by struggles among base leaders. Some aspired to structure the CUT so that local unions would have more power and participation within the national organization; others sought to limit their roles so that they could be more independent members of the confederation. Such fragmentation is magnified because of deep divisions within the CUT's leadership between those who tend toward confrontational measures (strikes and protests) to affect change, and those who prefer dialogue (with both management and the government).[18]

The few women's identity groups which remain extant join functional organizations in undergoing a process of fragmentation. In regards to the national level, the women's movement has disintegrated, but some organizations remain. Those that persist function as independent atoms, with few linkages between each other, and to other types of organizations or political parties. A commonly heard phrase asserts that "there are women in movement, but no women's movement now."[19] Chapter 6 details how the emergence of SERNAM, the pressures of society, and the strategies chosen by leaders have led to the fragmentation and de-mobilization of the women's movement.

Even the *centros de madres* (mother's centers, CEMA), albeit already defined as territorial organizations, have become more localized since the return to democratic rule. The national network of CEMA-Chile has fragmented, leaving the individual centers to function largely without national direction. The democratic government under Aylwin slashed CEMA's annual budget by 40% in 1991.[20] Up until that point, the *centros de madres* had received one hundred percent of their funding from the state. As budget cuts required each center to secure a portion of its own funding, they became more independent and distanced from the national organization. Under the new democracy, the government also disassembled the national network connected to CEMA; its traditional sister-organization, the *Voluntariado* (women's volunteer-pool), was disbanded, and the *Centros Abiertos* (child-care centers) were placed under separate administration. Each CEMA now functions largely as its own entity, making decisions based upon the needs of the community and participants, with few vertical links to the national organization.[21] This represents a significant change from the hierarchical format of the CEMAs under the military regime.

This phenomenon of localization manifests itself in the far corners of civil society, well beyond the realm of our chosen case studies. The youth are a crucial additional case to explore because they are the most extreme example of organizational localization. Among student groups, the focus has moved from protests against the authoritarian regime and state social policies to issues more specific to university life.[22] Before the transition to democracy, student organizations were either pro-Pinochet (like the Chilean Student Federation, FESECH) or against the dictatorship (like the Center of Students, CE). Now student organizations claim the participation of members from a variety of backgrounds and positions. For example, "it used to be that working with the CE meant working against the government and in solidarity with the *pobladores*. Now it means very little with respect to national politics. We have too much to worry ourselves here (on the campus/at the university)."[23] Student government organizations now focus on cultural activities, tuition issues, sports, university administration, career issues, student attitudes, communications, relations with businesses, and conferences with businesses and government ministries. Although the University of Chile's student paper continues to publish editorials on national politics, the CE's monthly newsletter has circulated only three commentaries on national politics since 1991. Furthermore, with the exception of the teacher's strikes in 1990 and 1991, the CE has not participated in any national movement since the return to democratic rule.

One of the most striking cases of localization after a transition to democracy occurred not in Chile, but in Argentina with the organization *Conciencia*. This group began as a pro-democracy, voter education organization and transformed as democracy re-emerged. As one of the leaders explained,

> After some years of successful achievements, we felt that certain societal patterns were changing and that we were failing to understand fully the nature of these changes. Through special research carried out with a private polling firm, we studied new strategies to reach more people with issues that really concern them. This led us to initiate our Friends of Parks and Municipalities programs, as we learned that people were primarily interested in solving immediate and local problems.[24]

Conciencia coupled localization with strategies bent on expanding into other parts of the Latin American region and on broadening its financial base.

It is interesting to note that the process of localization does not seem to be echoed in the actions of political parties. With social organizations having conceded national politics and campaigning, the parties appear entrenched in national level organizing. Although the municipal council members (*concejales*) are elected on party slates, the local party organizations have very little contact with the national party organizations. Ramon Farías, mayor of San Joaquín, explains in response to a question concerning ties to the national party structure, "we function as islands. Here (in the municipality) we have our own enemies, our funds, everything."[25] The linkages between parties and other citizens' organizations have also been ruptured. When parties initially re-emerged strongly and publicly in the late 1980s, they mobilized jointly with many social movement organizations to support the SI or the NO in the plebiscite, and then to back the presidential candidate of their choice in 1989. Now, both political parties and social organizations resist such ties, preferring to protect respectively their niches or autonomy from each other. A CUT leader interprets the parties' behavior as, "these days, the parties fear too much becoming involved in the labor movement...their fear, it seems to me, is related to receiving strong criticism from workers;" another explains the position of unionists, "Workers...must be autonomous from the parties, labor should have freedom from the viewpoint of its mission."[26] A labor scholar writes, "the idea of autonomous action from the parties and state...represents a common cultural patrimony of the labor movement" (Rojas, 1992: 256). Members interviewed from OEPs and women's groups expressed similar sentiments about the near-non-existence of party ties relative to the late 1980s.

Re-democratization has thus affected some groups in civil society by leading them to become more localized. Such a change in political environment causes organizations to focus many of their activities on the neighborhood level, leads the municipality to play a larger role in civil society, and fragments social movements to fragment. Organizations also begin to emphasize those issues and activities which are more immediate to their location or mission. The latter is highly interrelated with the move toward more particularism within civil society.

FROM SOCIAL MOVEMENT TO INTEREST ASSOCIATION

Civil society groups which survive a transition back to democracy are also likely to undergo a transformation of target; they move from being universalistic to particularistic. In other words, they transform themselves from social movement organizations into interest associations. The former encompasses organized efforts, often rooted in a common identity, to affect social change for a general, collective good.[27] Examples are the human rights movement, the women's movement, and the environmental movement. The latter denotes those organized efforts to organize or implement a change for which the primary beneficiaries are those participating. Microenterprises and lobbying groups are exemplary of interest associations. A Chilean government official explains this transformation,

Today, mobilization and participation are not seen as massive and
consistent demonstrations in the form of marches or protests, but
in a new style. It looks to mobilize people and communities in
those problems that directly concern them. For example, with
respect to women, it (the mobilization) tries to provide them with
awareness and to increase their capacity to react when faced with
domestic violence (as quoted in UNICEF, 1993: 119).

The reader will recall from Chapter 3 that the civil society organizations which continue to grow most rapidly following re-democratization are those which mobilize people around their direct interests
and communities, such as sports clubs, neighborhood associations, and senior citizens groups.

Why do many civil society organizations become more particularistic following re-democratization?[28] First, as discussed above
and in Chapter 4, a transition back to democracy leads to funding-
flight as the new government re-allocates its resources, and as
NGOs assume that the arrival of democracy means that their funds
are no longer as necessary. Organizations are faced with drastic
cuts in their budgets unless they become self-sufficient; this is
often the first step that a social movement organization takes
toward becoming an interest association. Second, the advent of
democracy permits organizations and members to focus on long-
neglected personal issues which were placed aside with the advent
of a "greater societal problem" (the dictatorship or communist infil-
tration, depending upon with whom you speak). Finally, adopting
a more particularistic approach may occur in response to a changing economic system. This reason is likely to dominate among civil
society groups in Eastern Europe, where they are attempting to
respond to simultaneous changes in both the economic and political systems. In the South American cases, such as Chile, the economic transformations preceded the political changes; thus this is
not the predominant reason for the rise of particularism in civil
society. Nevertheless, in Chile, civil society organizations must still
compete for members and funding under the guise of neo-liberalism.[29] Individualism and profit (or self-benefit), even among social
organizations, are becoming enticing codes words for potential participants and donors.

Organizations have thus become more particularistic. The focus of many groups is now on the education and capacitation of their members, as well social development and policies which will affect their membership. Over 20 percent of FOSIS funds are designated for the training and development of microenterprise groups (Petras and Leiva, 1994: 126). The director of FOSIS estimates that "approximately 90% or maybe 100%" of their proposals include some aspect which is aimed at tangible self-gain such as increasing income, providing goods, and improving education for the applicants and their memberships.[30] FOSIS has published a manual on *Promoviendo el Desarrollo Local* (Promoting Local Development, 1993) which teaches about leadership in organizations: how to hold a meeting, solicit opinions, lead a decision-making process. In the manual, the government argues that local development occurs mostly through community organizations. The following are two examples in which specific organizations have transformed to become more particularistic; note that many of these cases could also have been considered under the localization section.

During the 1980s, the OEPs devoted much of their time and energy to national social movements bent on fighting against the dictatorship and educating the public on the status of hunger and poverty in the country. Such goals were aimed at improving the lot of the whole of Chilean society. Now their campaign is much more particularistic. The great majority of their programs either focus on providing tangible benefits to their families and their particular community, or on personal education. In addition to their continued food (*ollas comunes*) and workshop (*taller*) activities, OEPs now also hold seminars on domestic abuse, literacy programs, and household finance courses. In the unique cases of *Talleres Melipilla* and *Talleres Genesis*, their activities now also include bakeries staffed by their membership; exactly half of the revenue goes back into the bakery and organization, and the other half is divided amongst the participants, based upon the number of hours dedicated to the project.[31]

In the realm of labor, both individual unions as well as confederations have transferred their energies from participating in social movements interested in a collective good to focusing more on providing benefits for their membership. As one unionist explains,

"We concern ourselves with the worker and the workplace now."[32] The CUT, early in the Aylwin years, formed the CEDUC (*Corporación de Educación Sindical*) to train union leaders; it has been the biggest new budgetary item for the CUT since the transition back to democracy. The emphasis is not on teaching skills directly related to the job, but rather on training leaders, improving literacy, balancing personal finances, and learning effective union organizing skills. The goal, Bustos explains, is to "give power to the worker in the areas where he [sic] has not traditionally had power..."*nos tenemos que mejorar*" used to mean the country, now it means improve the union, give power to the unionist."[33] Since the transition, the CUT has put aside campaigns on behalf of the rest of society and instead has focused their demands and propositions to the government on minimum wage, working conditions, and more generally about labor reforms.

BROADENING THE SCOPE OF ORGANIZATIONS

Although it appears that organizational births are the exception after re-democratization, the continued existence of many groups can in part be attributed to the birth of new activities and domains of participation. The opening of the political system has signaled an aperture of opportunities for organizations. Some groups, therefore, are able to survive because they expand the scope of their domain — they move from focusing on a very few specific issues to addressing a greater variety, or domain, of topics. This, in turn, allows them to be attractive to many citizens, and to maintain their membership levels. It is the need to entice members as well as donors that causes some organizations to broaden their scope; this has occurred among both territorial and functional groups. It is, however, the least common type of transformation I encountered while doing field research.

Juntas de Vecinos are the only type of organization among which broadening of domain is the most visible form of transformation. Neighborhood councils have expanded the scope of their activities in response to community needs and potential funding sources. For example, in Providencia the *Juntas* used to focus primarily on issues related to community recreation: decorations, parks upkeep, adult social events. With a grant from the municipality, they started in 1991 an annual toy-drive and Christmas party for children living in the neighborhood as well as for the children of those employees who work in the community. The impulse for such a project stemmed not only from the available funds, but also from an identifiable need. The new democratic government slashed CEMA's budget and re-organized the *Centros Abiertos*, rendering many of their projects (such as the children's party and toy-drive) unfeasible. The *Juntas* chose to take on those activities. Another arena into which *Juntas* have moved is that of vigilance. Traditionally, community safety and protection has been the domain of the police (or security forces during the dictatorship). With common crime significantly on the rise in post-authoritarian Chile, the *Juntas* have begun neighborhood vigilance programs. In the municipality of Pedro Aguirre Cerda, the *Juntas* met with both the municipal officers as well as the local police to design their role in community safety.[34] In Providencia, a few neighborhood councils merely assumed the responsibility themselves. In both cases, *Juntas* have taken on the responsibilities of posting signs reminding motorists to slow down, organizing "night watches" to patrol the neighborhood, and holding community meetings to educate citizens on how to secure their home and belongings.[35]

Some OEPs, in lieu of becoming more particularistic, have transformed into more educative or service organizations. They have moved from being focused on two specific goals —supplementing their food and income levels, and ending the authoritarian rule — to a more general mission of personal and community well-being. As detailed above and in Chapters 4 and 6, some OEPs have expanded their activities to include workshops on finances, domestic life, abuse, and literacy; community service projects in the form of school lunch programs or senior citizen centers have also begun to proliferate among OEPs. An interesting and illustrative case of domain transformation is found among *huertos*. *Huertos* traditionally function as communal gardening groups, focused on providing produce for the benefit of their members. Throughout the dictatorship, they were the most particularistic of the OEPs. Yet in a few unique cases, *huertos* have broadened their domain to become less interested in self-benefit, and more attuned to community education and environmental service. This reverse transformation was motivated, again, by the need to maintain membership levels and attract funds. When funding-flight coupled with an improved economy led the communal gardening groups to experience a decrease in members and resources, they broadened the scope of their activities so as to attract more participants and donors. Just as in the United States, the environment is currently a "sexy" topic in the southern cone. In the municipality of Puente Alto, *huertos* are diverging from their traditional functions to implement a tree-planting campaign along the principal streets and open spaces; they have also begun to broaden their scope to include public education projects about nutrition, as well as workshops on respecting the environment.[36] It appears that the inverse relationship is also beginning to emerge; environmental groups traditionally focused on affecting national policy in Chile have recently begun local projects to educate citizens on the environment, recycling, and the value and vulnerability of "natural patrimony."

MUNICIPALIZATION

The single factor which has most influenced the preceding three types of organizational transformation is the process of de-centralization, known throughout Latin America as municipalization.[37] In general terms, de-centralization is the transfer of power to inferior levels within a hierarchy (Irarrázaval, 1993: 9). In Chile, the *Ley Orgánica Constitucional de Municipalidades* of 1988 (Law #18.695; implemented in 1990) provided for the devolution of power from the historically strong executive branch to the local governments (municipalities), including administrative, financial, social and political responsibilities. Practically, this means that the municipalities expanded from being in charge of local transportation, street cleaning, and public spaces, to also administrating local schools and health clinics, funding social programs, and organizing community events. The process of municipalization included a change in the 1980 Constitution which now allows for the election of municipal leaders, and the use of plebiscites to gauge local opinion.

There are several arguments in favor of de-centralization which positively effect civil society. First, it strengthens democracy by allowing citizens to scrutinize the municipality more closely; they thus become more involved in local politics through plebiscite votes and public hearings. Second, it increases bureaucratic efficiency by eliminating many of the intermediary offices in the government hierarchy, and by allowing decisions to be made at the level at which they will be implemented. Third, funds granted through the municipality to civil society groups aid in getting people more involved in resolving their economic and social problems; this is particularly important because the state has proven somewhat incapable, due to financial and administrative factors, of resolving all of them.[38] Although the success and extent of Chile's municipalization program is still under dispute,[39] at the very least it has positively affected the incentives and opportunity structure for local participation.

The process of municipalization also often includes a parallel transfer of functions from the state to civil society. The state requests local groups to work together with the municipality to take on the conception and implementation of development initiatives. The strongest links between the municipality and social organizations have traditionally been found among the *Juntas* and the CEMAs; but with the increased funding and opportunities available through de-centralization, other groups such as sports clubs and subsistence organizations are now participating in local development and planning. The local level is thus converted into the arena where social actors are beginning to function in a partnership with the municipality and the state.

CONCLUDING COMMENTS ON TRANSFORMATION

In summary, in addition to the de-politicization phenomenon discussed in the previous chapter, there are three other ways in which organizations adapt to a change in their political environment. Civil society groups respond to a return to democratic rule by becoming more local and more particularistic, as well as by broadening the scope of their activities. They do so as a means of adapting to the constraints brought on by re-democratization: a scarcity in funding, a lack of a nationally compelling issue behind which to unite, and the competition with emerging political parties for resources and members. Organizations have also modified their activities and discourse in response to the government's neo-liberal policies.

I have one final explanation to offer for organizational transformation. After so many years of dictatorial rule, individuals have seemingly become unaccustomed to activating their citizenship through participating in the state or mobilizing around issues considered to be in the state's domain. Because such exercises were largely prohibited and severely repressed under the dictatorship, many citizens learned to steer clear of that which was related to politics and the state. They learned that local, non-political and community-oriented participation was safe — an arena in which they risked little fear of reprisal. Localized participation is therefore not only due to environmental constraints, but also can be considered to be learned behavior.

Organizations have outlived the return to democracy by recycling — or transforming — themselves in ways which are adaptive to their environment. The preceding chapters have established what happens to most organizations after re-democratization and why those changes occur; now let us explore what occurs with the unique case of women's organizing.

Notes

1. Luís Marín, Director of Community Development, Municipality of Pudahuel, interview with the author, August 23, 1994. Pudahuel is a lower-income *comuna* (municipality) in the western zone of Santiago.

2. Verónica Matus, head of the women's department of the Chilean Human Rights Commission, interview with the author, August 9, 1994. "*Mirándose al umbligo*" translates as "staring at our belly button;" it can also be taken as "twiddling our thumbs" or "immersed in ourselves."

3. This position could also be presented in terms of environmental constraints in lieu of organizational choice, by arguing that constraints on resources and membership drive organizations out of the national arena.

4. Ricardo Arabe, Director of FOSIS, interview with the author,
September 4, 1994.

5. Statistics published by the Chilean government, 1994, in
"Realizaciones y proyecciones del gobierno." Other data as cited by Hugo Larías V.,
Director of FOSIS, interview with the author, September 4, 1994. The
Chilean government has not had much of a policy on participation and
social organizations. A MIDEPLAN (1992) report states that there is a "lack
of a global definition of the forms in which social participation should be
operationalized from the perspective of government action."

6. On the fragmentation of social movements following a transition to
democracy, see Mainwaring (1987). He also argues that in the Brazilian
case, movements fragmented because the state intentionally pursued policies to that end; this does not seem to have occurred (yet) in Chile.

7. Each question was asked separately; participants ranked their
opinions of each office according to "much confidence", "not much, not little confidence", "no confidence" and "don't know or no response".
Therefore, the opinion total of each respective organization totals 100%.
Survey completed and presented by CENPROS, 1994.

8. In our final interview, I revealed to Winnie Lira my theory about the
four types of transformation. Without hesitation, she identified "localization" and "particularization" as the most common among OEPs, estimating
that 80% undergo the former, and of particularization, all of them experience it — "if they don't provide for themselves, *pués...chau*." Lira is the
Director of Fundación Solidaridad, and is the person who likely knows
more on a practical level than anyone else about OEPs in Chile. In interview with the author, September 7, 1994.

9. These reasons as discussed in meetings of *Taller Libertador* and *Olla
Pudahuel Norte* #2; observation by author, July and August 1994.

10. As estimated by Winnie Lira, in interview with the author on
September 7, 1994; see also Valdes et al, 1993b: 112.

11. As recounted to me by the members of *olla común Pudahuel Norte*
#2, during the month of July 1992.

12. *"Valpo"* is the slang term for Valparaíso, the port city in which the
Chilean Congress is located.

13. Luís Marin, Director of Community Development for Pudahuel,
confirms that the OEPs solicited suggestions from the municipality. He
says that their recommendations were a senior center, or a youth center

aimed at combating the drug and glue-sniffing problems in the community. Interview with the author, August 23, 1994.

14.   For more on programs in which *ollas comunes* take on the feeding and care of children and the elderly, see Fernandez (1994).

15.   See section below in which I expound upon the linkages between labor unions and political parties.

16.   Robinson Gaete, General Secretary of FETRASER; and Hugo Arancibia, President of FEREPA. As cited in Hernandez and Rojas (1992: 255).

17.   Bustos, in interview with the author, July 29, 1994.

18.   As opposed to the waning power and cohesion of the CUT's national level organization, the regional union structures have gained power. Within the CUT, the zonal and regional entities are being defined as active participants and instigators of regional development (see Frías, 1992: 25).

19.   A phrase commonly heard among women participants in Chile; first repeated to me by Verónica Matus, Director of the Women's Division of the Chilean Human Rights Commission, interview with the author, August 9, 1994.

20.   As cited in interview with Bertita Benavente, former vice-president of the *Voluntariado* (volunteer organization for CEMA), in interview with the author on August 17, 1994.

21.   The *Centros Abiertos* passed on to be part of a new governmental agency called INTEGRA. As recounted to me by Bertita Benavente, op. cit.; and Eliana Espinosa, founding member of the *Voluntariado*, interview with the author, August 5, 1994.

22.   Of course, this transformation of student groups may be seen as a process of localization and/or depoliticalization (as discussed in Chapter 4).

23.   Rodolfo Larrea V., President of the FECH (Student Federation of Chile), interview with the author, August 3, 1992.

24.   Martini as quoted in Diamond, 1992: 43.

25.   In interview with the author, July 13, 1994. Farías is a member of the Christian Democratic Party (PDC).

26.   First cite: Arturo Deig, President of the CUT in Concepción. Second cite: Waldo Aránguiz, President of the Metropolitan Construction Union. Both as quoted in Echeverría and Rojas (1992: 251, 253).

27.   With the onslaught of New Social Movement theory, there are several available definitions of a social movement. One which I find help-

ful is, "a form or network of collective action based in solidarity and a common identity, that develops a conflict or project, and pushes the boundaries of the structure of society in which it functions" (Melucci quoted in Valdés, 1989: 236). See also Touraine (1989 and 1987).

28.   See following section for the unique example of an organization (*huertos*) which has actually become less particularistic since re-democratization.

29.   For more on the neo-liberal system in Chile, see Petras (1994, chapter 3); and "Chile's Economic Miracle," in The Economist, week of June 6, 1994.

30.   Ricardo Arabe, Director of FOSIS, interview with the author, September 4, 1994.

31.   Fernando Mejia, Director of PROSAN, interview with the author on August 20, 1992; Maria Fecci, *olla* participant, interview with the author August 22, 1992; Tina and Silvia, members of Talleres Genesis, interviews with the author, August 3, 1994.

32.   Abelino Quilaqueo Peralta, Treasurer of the *Sindicato de Trabajadores Cecinas Super*, interview with the author, August 10, 1994.

33.   In interview with the author on July 29, 1994.

34.   During 1993 and 1994, the police participated in various programs aimed at encouraging more cooperation between them and neighborhood organizations; the goal is for citizens to assume a greater role in issues related to their security. In 1993, the state began funding more than one thousand municipal projects to improve local safety. See Augusto Varas and Claudio Fuentes, "*Carabineros de Chile: La función policial y la seguridad ciudadana*," Santiago: FLACSO-Chile, 1994.

35.   Information gathered in interviews, as previously cited, with Godoy (1994), Leal (1992), Rodriguez (1994), Vergen (1992), and two anonymous members of the Providenicia neighborhood council. The neighborhood association of Providencia had some involvement with "vigilance" in the 1980s. Members were encouraged to be aware of "that which might cause damage to our neighborhood, our neighbors, or *mi General*" (anonymous interviews, August 1992 and 1994). Such vigilance was akin to being political "watchdogs;" far different than the current community protection programs now being implemented by *Juntas*.

36.   Information from Maria Paz Ortega O., Secretary of Supplies, Puente Alto *huerto*, interview with the author on September 1, 1994; and

confirmed by Victor Montt, Office of Community Development, Puente Alto, interview with the author on September 3, 1994.

37.   For more on the specifics of de-centralization in Chile, see articles by Serrano, and Gonzalez, in Raczynski and Serrano (1992). For an argument that the Chilean de-centralization process has been nothing more than "mayor-ization" (giving power to the mayors, not to the entire municipality), see Muñoz Dálbora (1987). Over past two decades, many countries in Latin America have adopted decentralization programs, including Colombia, Chile, and Brazil. For comparative articles on de-centralization in Latin America, see Borja et. al. (1989) and Carrion et. al. (1991). A good theoretical article on de-centralization and democracy is Santana Rodriguez (1991).

38.   On this point, see especially Charlín (1992).

39.   See Raczynski and Serrano (1992), Carrion (1991), and Borja et. al. (1987).

Chapter Six

Barren Streets and Empty Households:

What Went Awry With Women's Organizing?

"We fought against the
repression and patriarchy
of Pinochet, but for women,
democracy is still patriarchal."[1]

From El Salvador to Venezuela to Argentina, the 1980s was a fren-
zied and politicized decade for women throughout Latin America.
They mobilized against authoritarian regimes and patriarchal systems, participated in subsistence cooperatives, and proposed new
legislation regarding divorce, reproductive rights and maternity
leave. Latin American feminist[2] groups grew in number as women
recognized that organizing around gender could lead to changes in
both their personal and political arenas. In that spirit, Chilean
women's groups teamed up with unions, human rights organizations, neighborhood associations and a host of other citizens'
groups in the 1970s and 1980s to push for an end to the authoritarian regime and to demand greater political rights and civil liberties. As wave of democratization swept the region, Chilean civil
society — and as part of that, feminist groups — reached their
highest levels of mobilization and organization to date. Previous
chapters have established that many organizations of civil society
can — and do — continue to mobilize and adapt to the environmental changes wrought by a transition to democracy.

I began this study with the belief that the organizations which would adapt to their new democratic environment most success-fully would be those whose members are connected not only through an issue or goal, but are also motivated by similarities among members or a common identity. Such groups should also have an advantage because they can use their identity as an addi-tional resource to win provisions and to mobilize members. Therefore, I initially believed that women's (and, in cases such as Guatemala and Brazil, ethnic) groups would adapt better to the transition than other organizations. Yet my research on women in Chile yielded a much more disturbing result. Feminist groups are the only generalizable category of organizations that have de-mobi-lized following the transition back to democracy in Chile; most other civil society groups have managed to survive re-democratiza-tion, at least in form if not in function. The ability of women's groups to use identity as a resource was not enough to enable them to overcome the obstacles often encountered in regime transitions. What went away with women's organizing?

The answer to this question is important because an accurate understanding of the new status of feminist organizations may yield much information about the resilience of civil society after democratization and about whether the emerging democracies are participatory for both sexes in Latin America.[1] It will indicate whether and at what levels women participate, how they articulate demands, and through which channels they interact with the state. Some scholars consider an active and dense civil society to be vital to the construction and maintenance of a stable democracy; there are those who build upon this, arguing that a democracy cannot be considered participative if women are not involved in the political system and power structure (Pateman, 1970). Citizens' organiza-tions such as feminist groups may act as a system of checks and balances on the state, serve as a learning ground for democratic principles, develop identities, provide outlets for the articulation of unrepresented demands, stimulate participation in the political process, and bolster the economic livelihood of their members.

In this chapter, I argue that there are five factors which adversely affect women's organizations after (re-)democratization and which may lead to their eventual disbanding: the youth and rigidity of their groups, a few ill-chosen strategies, the relationship of democracy to women, the state's institutionalization of women's issues, and an acute lack of funding. The implications of this phenomenon of demobilization are profound for women and feminism, for civil society, and for the (re-)emergence of the (Chilean) democratic regime itself.

HISTORICAL PATTERNS OF WOMEN'S ORGANIZING IN CHILE

The development of Chilean civil society in general, and among women's organizations in particular, was erratic under the prior democracy (pre-1973), with periods of stagnation interspersed with spurts of great momentum.[4] Women's first burst of participation came with the debate over suffrage. The 1925 Constitution provided for the much-resisted Social Laws (*Leyes Sociales*), giving increased rights to previously marginalized groups. Women were given the right to maternal leave, to serve as legal witnesses, and to administrate their own finances. The 1925 Constitution, however, stopped short of extending to them the right to vote.

In response to the continued disenfranchisement of women, the decades of the 1930s and 1940s in Chile were marked by a proliferation of women's organizations focusing on suffrage. With the founding of the *Movimiento Pro Emancipación de la Mujer* (MEMCH, Pro-Emancipation Movement of Chile) in 1935, many women's groups formed representing all sides of the political spectrum. Besides MEMCH, the *Segundo Comité Pro Derechos de la Mujer*, *Acción Cívica Femenina*, and the *Federación Chilena de Instituciones Femeninas*, among others, were constituted to take on the voting rights issue. Although the women participants would not have self-identified as belonging to such groups due to societal stigmatisms, these groups were part of a widespread middle- and upper-class feminist movement in which feminists questioned the way women were inserted into the social structure of the country; nevertheless, their questioning did not extend much beyond the electoral system.

Notably, in contrast to other citizens' organizations, these feminist groups enjoyed absolute autonomy from the political parties. It seems that this was the case because no one knew for which political tendency the majority of women would vote; the parties, therefore, chose to avoid the risk and uncertainty of the women's vote, and did not enter into the suffrage movement. Thus, the suffrage movement remained an isolated, but powerful sector of civil society; it was, in fact, the only citizens' sector prior to 1973 which gained significant autonomy from the parties.

The suffrage movement provoked women to leave their households to organize; for most women, this was their first such venture. In 1944, International Women's Day (March 8) was first celebrated in Chile, and in that same year, the first Chilean Women's Congress was held with nearly 500 women. The unity of women around this one issue paid off. In 1934, women received the right to vote in municipal elections; and in 1949, they won the right to vote in national elections (*Diario Oficial* law #9.292).

This triumph was followed by a period in which there occurred a marked decline in women's organizing. As organizations were unable to re-focus their energies toward new goals, and as women began to feel that their participation was less necessary since their interests were supposedly going to be represented by the political parties, they abandoned their groups and either became incorporated into the parties or returned to their households. Those that chose the former route were largely relegated to participating in the Women's Department of the parties. This began a thirty year period which Chilean feminist Julieta Kirkwood (1986) terms *"el silencio feminista"* ("the feminist silence"), when women ceased to be political actors and instead acted in the political sphere only in the role of wife or mother, or as a pawn of political parties.[5] This de-mobilization of women's groups in the 1950s issued a forewarning, although one which went apparently unheeded, to the Chilean feminist movement four decades later.

A second burst in women's participation occurred during the years (1970-1973) of President Salvador Allende's Popular Unity (*Unidad Popular*, UP) government and its experiment with socialism. During the years of Allende, between October 1972 and March 1973, the cost of living in Chile increased by 76.2 percent. Of three thousand basic products, over five hundred were unavailable in the stores and citizens waited in line for hours for their food rations. Prices on the black market skyrocketed beyond the reach of the lower and middle classes (Whelan 1989: 315-403). In December of 1971, thousands of women — perhaps the largest women's demonstration in Chile up to that point — took to the streets to protest the food shortages and long lines. They did so by carrying pans and banging on pots (hence it was labeled "The March of the Pots and Pans [Caserolas]") to symbolize the hard times which had befallen their kitchens, and by extrapolation, their households and country. It was, in fact, these women's marches together with multiple union strikes which first led the opposition's uprising against Allende.[6] With the fear, repression and laws that accompanied the military coup of September 11, 1973, women's organizations were again banished from the public sphere and most disbanded.

In 1973, immediately following the military coup, the Association of Democratic Women (*Agrupación de Mujeres Democráticas*) was started to support families repressed by the military government and to denounce human rights violations. Popular economic organizations (*organizaciones económicas populares*, OEPs) then sprung up in the late 1970s. Recall from previous chapters that "OEP" is the term used in Chile for those groups that began to arise out of a need to supplement their household income or food levels, and in some cases to protest the dictatorship. Examples of OEPs are soup kitchens (*ollas comunes*), artisan workshops (*talleres productivos*), shopping cooperatives (*comprando juntos*), and communal planting groups (*huertos*). OEPs were, and continue to be, almost exclusively comprised of women. These women were, in large part, on the political left or center; although it was not politics, but concern for the economic survival of their households which first prompted women to organize. Because many of their husbands had been "disappeared" or exiled by the military government, or they had been left unemployed by the neo-liberal economic policies, many women found themselves to be the head of the household. The OEPs offered them food and income supplements, and an opportunity to address the political roots of their problems. Although the OEPs occasionally participated in a joint project with the neighborhood councils, or co-organized a march with the unions or feminist groups, they functioned with complete autonomy from political parties and the state. In doing so, they were in a position to question both the existing political and economic systems. As one scholar observes, "By creating the need for alternative economic survival strategies, the (Pinochet) regime's economic policies have impelled women to organize. Similarly, the political crisis has mobilized women around human rights issues".[7]

Indeed, like no other time since the suffrage movement, the military regime prompted women to mobilize in a third burst of participation. At the height of anti-authoritarian organizing in 1987, there were thought to be around 11,000 women's groups in Chile (Silva Donoso, 1987). For many women in Chile as well as throughout Latin America, these anti-authoritarian organizations were their first participative ventures outside of the home or church; and often what began as a sewing cooperative or support group transformed into a means of voicing their political demands. Perhaps the most well-known example of women's organizing in Latin America is in neighboring Argentina; the Mothers of the Plaza de Mayo (*las Madres de la Plaza de Mayo*) formed in 1977 as a group of women protesting the tortures and disappearances of their loved ones. Their activities served to attract international attention to the atrocities of the Argentine military regime, and to mobilize domestic forces against it.

Not only did authoritarianism prompt a proliferation of groups which were largely comprised of women, but it also led to the genesis of innumerable feminist organizations. Beginning in the early 1980s in Chile, groups such as MOMUPO (*Movimiento de Mujeres Pobladoras*), *Casa de La Morada*, Feminist Movement (*Movimiento Feminista*, MF), *Mujeres de Chile* (MUDECHI), *Mujeres Por la Vida* (Women for Life) and others began to use issues of sanitation, economic equality, and social democracy to mobilize women into the public sphere in order to promote discourse on gender relations. The feminist groups used the International Women's Day (March 8) demonstrations as well as small seminars and educational pamphlets to unite women under a common banner: an end to authoritarianism and an end to patriarchy —these goals were portrayed as inextricably linked. Hindsight reveals that it was largely due to this linkage of issues that the feminist groups were able to rally such strong support in a society which heavily stigmatized feminism.[8] In fact, although the feminists cooperated with several of the political parties of the left (PC, PS, PPD, and to a lesser extent PDC) and cosponsored activities with the unions and OEPs, it seems that they were never well-incorporated nor well-connected with other institutions of civil society. Feminism and feminist groups were able to emerge from isolation only as part of the greater struggle against authoritarian repression.[9]

Women of the political right were also organized, although somewhat less visible, and decidedly non-feminist. These women took advantage of the already functioning corporatist structure of the CEMAs (*Centros de Madres*/Mothers' Centers), which were traditionally funded by the state, presided over by the president's wife, and run by volunteers (many of whom were married to military men). Although billed as a local center where women could interact and learn skills, the CEMAs were also used by those involved to mobilize women in defense of the military regime and a family-oriented, conservative life-style — everything which they perceived as being attacked by the OEPs and feminist groups.[10]   Therefore, CEMA combatted the feminist groups by teaching women that their place was in the home and with the children. Women were taught to find work that they could do in the house so as to remain with their family, and there was at least an implicit notion that women should support those who are advocates of the traditional family — the chief proponent in this realm was portrayed as Pinochet. Although such a political, pro-Pinochet agenda may have permeated the CEMAs, their daily activities were devoted to classes in crafts, personal hygiene, nutrition and child-care, as well as to the planning of social events. The CEMAs did not often participate in organizing outside of their neighborhood; the one exception is that once every year, the women of CEMA would hold a march to show their commitment to the *patria*, to promote unification among (conservative) women and to offer an alternative to feminist organizations.[11]

Women, particularly feminist groups and those reacting against them, were highly mobilized and well-organized during the second half of the authoritarian regime in Chile, a phenomenon also observable in many other Latin American countries in transition including Venezuela, Brazil, Argentina, Guatemala and El Salvador. How has the emergence of democracy, or re-emergence of it in the Chilean case, affected feminists' organized participation?   Have they faired worse or better than their civil society cohorts?

LEVELS OF ORGANIZATIONAL MOBILIZATION AMONG WOMEN

As the Chilean case study in Chapter 3 demonstrated, most civil society organizations do not disband after democratization. While their mobilization levels may decline sharply, their organizational levels tend to maintain a constant level; in other words, despite that fact that we rarely continue to see thousands of emotionally-charged protesters in the street, the organizations of civil society continue functioning quietly in the workplaces, neighborhoods and churches of post-democratization societies.

Yet *in marked contrast to the rest of civil society, feminist groups — or what I have termed "women's identity groups" — which flourished in the 1980s have either disbanded or become significantly weakened since the return to democratic rule.*[12] This argument is counter to my original hypothesis upon beginning field research, and as a woman who strongly identifies as a feminist, de-mobilization was an argument which I also normatively resisted. *Mujeres Por la Vida* (Women for Life) and MUDECHI (*Mujeres de Chile*), both active presences in the prior decade, have completely disappeared; their leadership positions, membership lists, organizational structure and offices have ceased to exist. MEMCH '83 (*Movimiento Pro-Emancipación de la Mujer Chilena*), which was first founded in 1935 and then experienced a re-birth in the early 1980s, will need to be resuscitated yet again if it is to be considered a functioning organization. MOMUPO (*Movimiento de Mujeres Pobladoras*) and the Feminist Movement (*Movimiento Feminista*, MF) now resemble ghost-towns; the organizational structures still exist, but there are virtually no inhabitants nor activity within them. *Casa de la Morada* and *Tierra Nuestra* persist as the strongest of the previously existing feminist groups in the post-transition phase; they have, however, lost much of their former intensity and capacity to mobilize. According to a co-director of *Tierra Nuestra*, around 1988 there were some 100 feminist groups with an average of 20 members each in their zone (the southern section of Santiago); as of 1994, there were 74 groups with an average of 15 participants.[13] The director of *La Morada* likewise acknowledges that the level of participation and commitment within her organization has dwindled noticeably since the transition back to democracy.[14] Both of these women's movement leaders, Gaviola and Olea, along with feminist scholar Levy (1992), agree that not only are many feminist groups dying in Chile since 1990, but also very few new organizations have been founded. This pattern of de-mobilization can also be found among women's groups on the political right, although to a lesser extent.

Similar patterns of organizational demobilization are found among the CEMAS (*Centros de Madres*/Mother's Centers). CEMA-Chile was founded in the early 1960s, by the state, to organize neighborhood women to learn skills which would be useful in the household. It evolved into an organization which taught women how to supplement their household income while remaining in the home, as well as a vehicle for encouraging women to maintain traditional gender roles and foster family values. It quickly grew into the largest citizens' organization in Chile. By 1974, there were approximately 20,000 CEMAs with nearly one million members. Yet in 1982 that number had dropped to 9,061 centers with 230,000 members. These numbers have continued to decrease slightly, even during the height of organizational mobilization in the 1980s; with the emergence of new women's organizations, some members abandoned CEMA. The sum total of CEMAs has now fallen below that of the democratic regime under Frei.[15]

The high levels of women's organizing in the political opposition during the 1980s led many to be optimistic about their future role under democracy. Yet at the present moment, women are weakly represented in leadership positions in the government, political parties and citizens' organizations. Furthermore, a substantial number of feminist groups and CEMAs have disbanded since the transition to civilian rule.[16] Such a phenomenon is counter to my original hypothesis about the survivability of identity groups; what went awry with women's organizing?

EXPLAINING THE DECLINE OF WOMEN'S IDENTITY GROUPS

Why has this phenomenon of de-mobilization occurred and largely confined itself to women's groups — particularly feminist groups?

The reasons are both exogenous and endogenous to the organizations themselves. In contrast to the other sectors of civil society which have survived re-democratization, women's organizations faced different environmental constraints and committed fatal strategic errors during the transition period. My research in Central America and Haiti indicates that these constraints and errors are not unique to women's groups in Chile.

First, feminist groups may be seen as "disposable" organizations. From the viewpoint of population ecology theory (within the field of organization theory),[17] organizational populations which are young and rigid are those most likely to disband in the face of extreme changes in the environment. This occurs because they have not built up a sufficient reserve of resources and knowledge to weather the inevitable period of uncertainty which accompanies environmental change. Organizations need time to pass through an evolutionary process through which the more robust and adaptable survive, or are "selected" by, their environment. As the change in political environment (the transition back to democracy) occurred in Chile, the population of feminist groups was among the youngest and most rigid in civil society. With the single exception of MEMCH, the unions, neighborhood councils and political parties had much longer organizational histories than the feminist groups. Although many of the former organizations were "re-born" during the return to democracy, they could rely upon resources, contacts, and learning which had, in effect, been "stock-piled" for the 17 years of relative inactivity during the dictatorship. Yet for women's empowerment groups, their birth in the 1980s marked the very genesis of their individual organizations, and the end of their population's hibernation begun in the early 1950s. Their youth and inexperience thus pre-disposed them to death when faced with significant transformations in the political system.

Also, much of this population perceives identity as something non-negotiable; in adopting this attitude, they are more likely to be inflexible or rigid to environmental changes. For example, although it might have been important for organizations to learn from each other, compromise, and share funds in order to survive, feminist groups were likely to avoid inter-dependent relations because of their preoccupation with issues of autonomy. As described by Ana Maria Arteaga, feminist groups are "very jealous of any outside intervention that might interfere with the management of their own organizations and worried about maintaining their identity and autonomy, these organizations operate, in general, in a very isolated and restricted environment."[18] Therefore, both rigidity and youth contributed to the "disposable" nature of the population.

Second, the strategies chosen by feminist groups were at times ill-conceived, leaving them vulnerable to the societal changes wrought by re-democratization. Because feminist issues are especially stigmatized throughout Latin America, many gender-related organizations have difficulty attracting members or funding. In response, feminist leaders in Chile chose to adopt a logical[19], although ultimately fatal, approach to this problem: they linked their women's identity issues with democratization — or more precisely, they associated their struggle against patriarchy with the fight against authoritarianism. "The search for human rights was tied to women's rights, and the analysis of military authoritarianism became a critique of authoritarianism in the family...Awareness of violence against women in prisons made it acceptable to talk about violence against women in the home and on the street" (Jaquette, 1989: 5-6). The problem arose not in the linking of issues (patriarchy to authoritarianism), but in the strategy taken. As presented by union leaders, their goal was "first, to re-establish a condition of personal human rights (democratic rule), and then resolve specific social problems (such as union issues)."[20] In other words, the workers were told that first they must defeat the dictatorship, and then the conditions would be right to push for greater labor rights; it was portrayed as a two-step process. Leaders of the women's movement, however, took a different approach. They tried to engender participation by presenting the struggle as a single-step process; the implication was that with the advent of democracy, women's rights would be achieved. Leaders organized marches with chants calling for "democracy in the country and in the home;" convocatorios (calls to assemble) issued by the women's movement claimed that "The conquest (achievement) of our full rights as women goes hand in hand with our liberation as a people." Linking the two issues raised unrealistic expectations among the members of feminist groups; it was a tactic which backfired because the achievement of the two goals did not coincide. Reflecting upon their strategy, many of the leaders of the women's movement concede that "we calculated badly and now we must recuperate."[21] The cost of the miscalculation indeed seems high; when the coming of democracy did not bring gender equality, many participants became disillusioned and stopped participating.

Not only the strategies chosen, but also the manner in which they were chosen, contributed to the de-mobilization of feminist groups. A new environment (in this case, a new political regime) usually necessitates a change in organizational tactics or goals; the process of arriving at those tactics or goals can be divisive for any group. In the case of *La Morada*, there occurred a *"gran pelea"* between two factions proposing conflicting strategies. That of Margarita Pisano wanted to continue with an aggressive activist approach focusing on national issues and policies; Raquel Olea and her supporters instead advocated activities more internal to the organization, emphasizing the development of identity, culture and communication among the women. The latter approach (and Olea) more or less won out, but not without a bitter struggle in which *La Morada* lost many of the women who had sided with Pisano. Although this internal struggle cost *La Morada* many members, it likely also accounts for its survival. Those organizations which did not transform their goals and organizational approaches to adapt to the new political environment, and instead continued with their old methods of participation, have disbanded. Explains one women's leader Verónica Matus,

> The problem among the women's groups is that they continued using the same methods of participation (under democracy) that they did under the dictatorship...everything in terms of demands and protests...assuming that *acción vale en si mismo*. It is like the child that is called to say grace or dance for her aunt. But really, that action looks good but gets you nothing.[22]

How, and which, strategies were chosen contributed to the de-mobilization of women's identity groups.

Third, both a theoretical and empirical argument can be made that the new political environment is inhospitable to these organizations; in other words, women and women's groups are not the "winners" in democracy. Many will argue that most democracies treat women as political equals, however, that equality is merely in a formal sense. The reality of women's citizenship under democracy runs counter to this notion of formal political equality. Women and women's organizations tend to lose in democracies because as a regime type, democracy seeks to divide the public and private realms. Politics and the contestation of power are considered to be in the public domain. Yet the gender division of labor usually relegates women to the private, and thus less powerful, arena. Pateman writes that "women as wives will largely be confined to (a) small circle...and so will find it difficult to use their vote effectively."[23] Women lack power in democracy because democracy demands that citizens be able to participate in elections and decision-making processes — but such activities are difficult to partake in without leaving the household. J. S. Mill claims that individuals must participate in a wide variety of public institutions in order to attain the necessary education for active, democratic citizenship. Yet with the traditional gender division extant in many newly democratizing countries, how can women attain equal citizenship from within the home?

The fact that the public and private spheres cannot be so cleanly divorced from each other only serves to further the subordinate position of women under democracy. Norms and relationships within the state become replications of those within the household; and conversely, relations within families often reflect a societal model. Why should the manner in which women and men interact in the public realm (as citizens) be any different than in the private realm (as family members)? Why should institutions (organizations or governments) dominated by men be empathetic or responsive to women's groups and demands? If patriarchal attitudes and relationships are embedded within the home and society, they will be replicated in voting patterns and decision-making processes on the state level. As Friedman (1998) argues, the political opportunity structure which emerges from democratization is gendered — meaning that it reflects the traditional division of power and labor. The fact that democracy formally considers women as political equals does nothing to urge voters or leaders to put aside their gender prejudices in order to elect or appoint women to positions of power. Voting patterns and decision-making processes will simply reflect those deep-seated biases. The assumption and rhetoric that democracy affords equal political status to all citizens serves only to mask the political inequalities which do exist between men and women.[24] As Pateman rightly asserts, even if women were given the opportunity to act as equal political citizens, they are likely not to be in a position to take advantage of it. As women enter the work force, they assume two jobs — as employee and as mother. Activating their citizenship by participating in the democratic process would mean taking on a third job. Until men become more involved in child-rearing, democratic participation and thus, involvement in organizations, will run as a distant third priority for many women.[25] This is clearly an issue not just of a lessening in women's participation, but also of a lack of representation as women's voices find few outlets in many democracies.

Empirically, women's leadership in the Chilean and the world arenas has not benefited from a transition back to democracy. Globally, despite the nearly 40 cases of democratization over the past decade, the percentage of elected women legislators has declined from 15% of the worldwide total in 1988 to 11% in 1994.[26] Following the Chilean transition, women still held only 16% of the directive posts in political parties in 1991, many of which were in the women's departments (Levy, 1992: 105). In other areas, the number of women in leadership positions is also strikingly low. Out of 334 mayors elected in 1994, 24 are women. Under Aylwin, out of 27 cabinet ministers, only one was a women. During the first three years of Frei, only three cabinet *ministras* and 2 out of 28 undersecretaries were women; there were only 9 women out of 120 *diputados*, and only 3 women out of 47 senators. There are no women on Chile's Supreme Court. Eighty-six percent (86%) of union offices are held by men; and in the national council of the largest labor confederation (the CUT/*Central Unitaria de Trabajadores*), 5 out of 59 directors are women. The new generation continues in the same strain, giving little hope for women in leadership; in student federations only 18.9% of the directors are women.[27] Similar trends exist in Bosnia, Haiti, and in many parts of Central America. These statistics, combined with the phenomenon of organizational de-mobilization, suggest that at the very least, democracy is somewhat inhospitable to women and their organizations.

Finally, women's empowerment groups also de-mobilize for reasons external to the organizations (beyond that of the environment itself). One example is that more than any other category of organizations in Chile, feminist groups have experienced a severe decrease in funding in recent years. For the most part, this is due to the coincidence of strong economic growth and the return to democracy; Chile has stopped being an international priority. Because Chile now appears to be a "success story," much of the pro-democracy or solidarity funding previously destined for its civil society groups has now been re-routed to help fledgling Eastern European organizations.[28] The funding situation has been difficult for almost all Chilean organizations since the transition back to democracy. But women's groups have especially suffered because much of their external funding was linked to both democratization and the United Nations' Decade of the Women (1975-1985), the latter of which brought in considerable resources to feminist groups. Unfortunately, the residual funds which carried over from that decade have since dried up for most women's identity groups. Many had hoped that the United Nations-promoted International Year of the Family (1994) would bring another resource boost to women's organizing in Latin America. Yet with some urging from the Catholic Church, the money was steered away from gender identity groups and funneled into more traditional and functional organizations, such as sewing cooperatives and neighborhood centers.[29] Faced with a significant decrease in resources, many women's empowerment groups have disbanded or have severely limited the scope of their activities.

The institutionalization of women by the state is another exogenous factor which has contributed to the de-mobilization of feminist groups. In response to women's demands which had surfaced during the presidential campaign, newly-elected President Patricio Aylwin created SERNAM in January of 1991 (by governmental decree) and appointed Soledad Alvear as the first director. A lawyer, and the only woman on Aylwin's cabinet at that time, she lacked experience with grassroots organizations and with the women's movement; Alvear, for both personal and job-related reasons, was conservative on many issues which were critical to feminists. Because it is a state agency, those in SERNAM are pressed to uphold the politics of the government, which often coincide with those of the Catholic Church: no abortion, no divorce, respect for the home and family. Therefore, SERNAM dismissed as too progressive many of the demands made by women's identity groups in civil society. Without the stamp of approval by SERNAM, it was difficult for women's groups to receive state funds or support; state aid was therefore denied at a vital time for these women's organizations as their other sources of funding were disappearing.

Many women with whom I spoke also argued that SERNAM monopolized some of the critical women's issues, like domestic violence, by presenting itself (to the legislature and the citizenry) as the only legitimate voice of Chilean women on the subject. Others interviewed expressed a more disturbing viewpoint: since the state was now committed to representing women's issues, it was no longer necessary for them to mobilize around those issues — their energy (i.e. participation) could be re-allocated elsewhere. It seems that forces external to feminist groups, in this case the creation of a state agency to institutionalize women's issues, have become an obstacle to women's organizing. As a leader of the women's movement explained, "SERNAM was a demand of the women, but ironically, it has led to the decline of the women's movement."[30] Such an experience with a national-level women's ministry may send up a warning flare to feminists in other countries, such as in Haiti, where similar experiments with women's ministries are just beginning. Waylen (1996) notes a related paradox: that ministries such as SERNAM take strength from the existence of women's organizations, but at the same time may be responsible for the decline in those groups.

In contrast to the feminist groups, the decline in CEMAs can be explained by way that CEMA had always been directed by the President's wife; the organization thus became highly linked with the military regime under the directorship of Lucía Hiriat de Pinochet during the 1970s and 1980s. When the authoritarian regime lost legitimacy, CEMA too lost legitimacy — and members. As a way of rejecting the Pinochet government, the emerging democratic regime instead chose to support women's organizing through the inception of a new state agency, SERNAM, and thereby drastically reduced the state resources available to CEMA-Chile.

LESSONS LEARNED

Women's groups, particularly feminist groups, appear to be the only generalizable category of organizations which have taken the path of de-mobilization following the transition back to democracy in Chile; most other groups have managed to survive re-democratization, at least in form if not in function. Contrary to what I had originally argued, the ability of feminist groups to use identity as a resource was not enough to enable them to overcome several destructive factors. *Their youth and rigidity, a few ill-chosen strategies, the relationship of democracy to women, the state institutionalization of women's issues, and an acute lack of funding — all instigated by democratization — have led feminist groups to de-mobilize.* Although I do not intend with this chapter to portray democracy as a societal ill, in the case of women's groups, it appears to be an organizational handicap. Those few feminist groups that survived democratization did so only by instituting deep, and often destructive, changes in their organization.

In Chile, it is oft-repeated that, "There are women in movement, but no women's movement now." Yet even "in movement," women as individuals are largely excluded or have withdrawn from the political power system in Chile. All too often, organizations are made up of mostly men, or they are based upon a male-dominated hierarchy. Leadership positions in unions, business associations, and neighborhood organizations go largely to men. Men are seen first as workers and second as fathers, and women are viewed in the reverse relationship. As long as all of these factors exist then women will not be able to participate equally in civil society and such a system, when women comprise over half over the citizenry, cannot be considered a participatory democracy. The implications of this, which are profound for women, for civil society and for the longevity of the democratic regime, are discussed in Chapter 7.

Is Chile a unique case, or are we likely to find a similar downward trend in women's organizing in other (re-)emerging democracies? Brazil and Venezuela's return trips to democracy also appear to have been accompanied by a parallel decline in women's groups (Friedman, 1998). Both experienced high levels of feminist mobilizing under authoritarianism followed by a disbanding of such groups when democracy re-appeared. The fact that these South American cases were all instances of re-democratization may call into question their generalizability; however, this study offers a forewarning to women's organizations within first-time transitions to democracy as well. While international actors may offer financial security, while government ministries may provide a channel of representation, and while promises of equality may attract new members, reliance on such mechanisms may assure short-term survival and success for an organization but it may also lay the groundwork for its eventual disbanding. If feminist groups hope not only to topple the dictatorships but also to function in the ensuing democratic systems, self-sufficiency, autonomy from the state and flexibility should be their chosen strategies. Women in newly democratizing countries, such as Haiti and Guatemala, would do well to heed the lessons learned by the *chilenas*.

Notes

1.   Olea, interview with the author, April 21, 1995, op. cit.
2.   The term feminism is used to denote those groups which organize around women's identity issues and whose primary goal is the empowerment of women (in groups and as individuals) through disbanding structures of oppression. It is akin to what I elsewhere term, "women's identity groups."
3.   If we were to be concerned with the consolidation of democracy solely during the current generation, studying organizational patterns of women's groups would be of less importance. However, because we are

interested in the long-term consolidation of democracy, which necessitates infusing political structures as well as successive generations with democratic values, the issue of gendered participation may be critical, especially in Latin America. In that region, values are mostly transmitted at home and in schools — by women. If women value democracy and participate in it, it is likely that future generations will as well. Therefore, identifying whether and how women are participating after democratization will help us to understand better the possibilities for current and future democratic consolidation.

4.   See Chapter 2 for a more general and historical overview of civil society organizing in Chile.

5.   On the women's suffrage movement and its after-effects in Chile, see the overview by Patricia Chuchryk," in Jaquette (*ibid*, 1994b, chapter 3); Natacha Molina, *Lo feminimo y lo democrático en el Chile de hoy*, Santiago: Centro de Estudios y Económicos Sociales, 1986, chapter 2; and María de la Luz Silva Donoso, *La participación política de la mujer en Chile: las organizaciones de mujeres*, Buenos Aires: Fundación Friedrich Naumann, 1987, chapter 3.

6.   For a detailed overview of the motivations and means of women's organizing under Allende, see Elsa Chaney, "The Mobilization of Women in Allende's Chile," in Jane Jaquette (ed.), *Women in Politics*, New York: John Wiley & Sons, 1974, pp. 267-279; and María de los Angeles Crummett, "El Poder Femenino: The Mobilization of Women Against Socialism in Chile," *Latin American Perspectives*, volume 4, number 4, 1977, pp. 103-113.

7.   Citation from Chuchryk in Jaquette, op.cit. The singular best overview of the OEPs is Luis Razeto et al, Las organizaciones económicas populares, 1973-1990, Santiago: PET, 1990; excellent articles on OEPs by Roberto Urmeneta, Jaime del Pino and Margarita Fernandez appear in issues of *Economía y Trabajo*, Santiago: PET, 1991-1994. The most reliable source of statistics and analysis of the OEPs is the *Programa de Economía del Trabajo* (PET) in Santiago, Chile.

8.   Olea (1992: 30) explains how feminists were able to link issues under military rule to gain public support: "*cuerpo de resistencias a las ordenanzas militares, condiciones de quiebres; de expresion extremada del poder patriarcal, de despliegue desbordado del autoritarismo de la razón masculina.*"

9.   The re-birth of the feminist movement in Chile is an interesting tale; details may be found in Silva Donoso, op.cit. and Molina, op.cit. On the rise, fall and subsequent re-constitution of MEMCH, see its own pub-

lication, "MEMCH, Antología para una historia del movimiento fememino en Chile," Santiago: MEMCH, 1983.

10.   The military government also sought to organize and influence men in a similar manner through the DIGEDER (General Directorate of Sports), which was funded by the state but run by volunteers, and aimed almost exclusively at male citizens.

11.   CEMA is the one case in this research which does not fit nicely into the civil society box. CEMA was not a self-constituted organization; it was founded and organized by the Chilean government in the 1950s. On the national level, its funding comes from the state, as well as from international donations, and its leaders are closely connected to the state. However, on the local level, the role of the government is very ambiguous and distant; the neighborhood CEMAs were entirely run by volunteers. For this reason, and because it is the most visible and wide-reaching example of women's organizing on the political right, it is included as one of the cases in this study.

12.   Recall from Chapter 1 that women's identity groups are often, although not always, synonymous with feminist groups. Also, with the exception of women's identity groups, Chilean civil society is basically devoid of other identity organizations; for example, there are very few ethnic groups or gay/lesbian groups.

13.   Eda Gaviola, co-director of *Tierra Nuestra*, interview with the author, August 25, 1994.

14.   Raquel Olea, director of *La Morada*, interview with the author, April 21, 1995. There is no other hard time-series data on women's identity groups in Chile.

15.   Teresa Valdés and Marisa Weinstein, *Mujeres que sueñan: las organizaciones de pobladoras en Chile 1973-1989*, FLACSO: Santiago, 1993, pp. 56, 99. For more information on CEMA-Chile, and the debate about whether women joined out of interest or because they felt pressured by the government to do so, see Chuchryk in Jaquette (1994b), Kirkwood (1986), and Molina (1986).

16.   I am compelled to note that more than any other category of organizations, it is exceedingly difficult to judge the level of organized participation after re-democratization in the case of women's identity groups. The sparse data on these organizations is characterized by the inexistence of a national center for keeping such information. Since most women's groups fall neither under the heading of functional nor territorial organiza-

tions, they are not required to register for *personalidad jurídica* (legal status granted by the state to functional and territorial groups) therefore, the INE (*Instituto Nacional de Estadisticas/* National Institute of Statistics) has kept no official statistics on them. Additionally, women's groups themselves have not maintained reliable records of their organizations over time. According to Teresa Valdés and Enrique Gomáriz ("Mujeres latinoamericanas en cifras: avance de investigación, Chile," Documento de Trabajo, FLACSO: Santiago, 1992, p. 71), the women participants do not see the importance of keeping such data; nor do they see a connection between this information and collective identity, nor between collective identity and the development of the women's movement. They also fail to recognize how their organization's history might be used as a resource in attracting members and funding, as well as in fostering identity. More practically, women's identity organizations are usually progressive (or feminist) in nature and hence are associated (and often, associate themselves) with the political left. Since many such groups met with severe repression during the years of the dictatorship, it was an issue of personal safety which kept many of the women from keeping extensive records of their activities and membership.

17.   For the arguments on population ecology theory, see Michael T. Hannan and John Freeman, "The Population Ecology of Organizations," *American Journal of Sociology*, March 1977, pp. 929-64; Glen R. Carroll, "Organizational Ecology," *Annual Review of Sociology*, 1984, pp. 71-93; and Howard E. Aldrich, *Organizations and Environments*, Prentice Hall, 1979. Carroll believes that the population ecology arguments can also be applied to individual organizations, in addition to populations of organizations.

18.   Quoted from Arteaga, "Politización de lo privado y subversión de lo cotidiano" in *Mundo de Mujer*, Centro de Estudios de la Mujer: Santiago, 1994. Not only is this an example of organizational rigidity, but it also illustrates how strategies of organizations can lead to their demise. This phenomenon of isolation was partially by choice of the organizations, and partly by imposition of society. Although women left the household to organize in the early 1980s, they (women's identity groups) never really occupied public space. Society did not let them "in" because of the stigmatism against feminism. Therefore, the women's groups did not form interdependent relationships with other components of civil and political society, and women were unable to claim permanent leadership in most of the traditionally "male" domains. For more on the issue of public versus

private realms, see Carole Pateman, *The Disorder of Women: Democracy, Feminism and Political Theory*, Polity Press, 1989, chapter 6.

19.   I say "logical" because, as Julieta Kirkwood (1986, op.cit.) argues, with authoritarianism women "are, in a certain manner, faced with a known phenomenon: authoritarianism as a culture is their daily experience."

20.   Manuel Bustos, President of the CUT, as quoted by Bascuñán Echeverría and Jorge Rojas Hernández (*Añoranzas, Sueños, Realidades: dirigentes sindicales hablan de la transición*, Ediciones SUR: Santiago, 1992, p. 15); and elaborated on in author's interview on July 29, 1994. See also Jorge Rojas Hernández ("Desafíos estructurales del movimiento sindical chileno en el proceso de transición a la democracia," in Echeverría and Rojas, *ibid*, 1992, p. 237) who argues that "the end of the dictatorship was perceived as the prior and fundamental condition to the achievement of their (unions') own interests."

21.   Interview with Olea, April 21, 1995. Also as stated by Verónica Matus (head of the women's department of the Chilean Human Rights Commission, interview with the author, August 9, 1994), "...we put too much weight on our overly-high expectations...We thought we were making great strides not only in ending the dictatorship, but also in women's rights. There seemed to be so many of us...Now I realize that we were just a very small part of it."

22.   Matus, interview with the author, August 9, 1994. "*Acción vale en si mismo*" translates to "action in and of itself is worthwhile."

23.   Pateman, op.cit., 1989, pp. 216-7.

24.   This argument serves to explain Raquel Olea's comment with which this chapter opened. For more on feminism and democracy see Anne Phillips, "Must Feminists Give Up on Liberal Democracy?" *Political Studies*, vol. XL, 1992, pp. 68-82.

25.   On the double responsibilities of "working mothers" and their lack of time for democratic involvement, see Z. R. Eisenstein, *The Radical Future of Liberal Feminism*, New York: Longman Press.

26.   Statistic is for elected legislators and parliamentarians. Source: UNICEF, "The Progress of Nations," 1995.

27.   Statistics from Eugenia Hola and Gabriela Pischedda, *Mujeres, Poder y Política*, Centro de Estudios de la Mujer: Santiago, 1993, pp. 64-7. For an argument on why so few women hold elected office in democracies, see M. M. Lee, "Why Few Women Hold Public Office: Democracy and Sexual Roles," *Political Science Quarterly*, no. 91, 1976, pp. 297-314.

28.   In the early 1990s, much of the funding was headed to Poland and the Czech Republic; more recently there has been a dramatic shift toward the former Yugoslavia. See Chapter 4 for a more detailed account of the "funding flight" problem.

29.   As argued by Rosita Equinolas, co-director of Tierra Nuestra, "The (Catholic) Church and the government used it (the U.N.'s International Year of the Family) to push women back into their traditional roles" (interview with the author on August 25, 1994).

30.   Quotation is that of Raquel Olea, director of *La Morada*, interview on April 21, 1995; sentiment was also expressed by Eda Gaviola, co-director of *Tierra Nuestra*, interview on August 25, 1994. For more on the tensions within, and concerning, SERNAM and the women's movement, see Chuchryk in Jaquette (op.cit., 1994b; particularly 137); Matear (1997); and Waylen (1996).

CHAPTER SEVEN

Surfing the Democratization Wave:

A View of Post-Transition Civil Society

> *From a means, organization
> becomes an end.*[1]

> *La politique en Amérique
> Latine se définit plus en
> termes de participation
> - ou de non-participation -
> que de représentation.*[2]

Organized participation has outlived the transitions back to democratic rule in Latin America. The preceding chapters have demonstrated that most organizations adapt to their changing political environment by transforming their foci, goals, and operating procedures to reflect the environmental changes. As a society moves away from authoritarianism toward democratic rule, groups tend to become more particularistic, more localized, less politicized, and broader in scope, following what I term to be a path of "transformation."

As demonstrated through the case of Chile, the hypotheses and research results of this study do not sustain either of the two strands of conventional wisdom in contemporary literature on participation and democratization. The first, put forth by Huntington (1968), posits that the emergence of a democratic regime signals the opening of political channels. When this is coupled with an improvement in socio-economic levels, citizens will increase their social and political aspirations. These aspirations will lead them to higher levels of mobilization that, it is argued, will put too much pressure on the state. If such participation is not institutionalized (Huntington suggests through political parties), it can de-rail the democracy. The evidence presented in this study suggests that Chile may be heading in a direction distinct from that hypothesized by Huntington.[3] Chile underwent a return to democratic rule just as it experienced a resurgence of economic growth. Yet mobilization levels did not significantly increase after the arrival of democracy, nor did citizens place more demands on the state. In fact, the data show that most organized participation now occurs outside of the realm of the state, and political parties do not boast high levels of control over organized participation.

The second hypothesis in the literature, forwarded by O'Donnell and Schmitter (1986), asserts that after the peak of a transition to democracy, mobilization levels crest and begin to diminish significantly while groups de-politicize. This is said to occur because of the emerging competition between organizations and political parties, a shortage of resources, and a disillusionment of the citizenry with democracy. While all of these variables indeed exist, the data do not support O'Donnell and Schmitter's suggested drop in participation levels (what I term "de-mobilization"); to the contrary, the data that are available indicate that organizations continue to exist and follow a path of transformation, with the notable exception of women's identity groups as detailed in Chapter 6. It appears that, on the whole, organizations and their members continue participating; it is the object of that participation which changes. This occurs not just in cases of re-democratization, but also in first time transitions to democracy. Yet O'Donnell and Schmitter's hypotheses are not entirely off the mark. The evidence presented in Chapter 4 sustains their claim that groups become less overtly political after a transition back to democracy as they begin to emphasize more economic and particularistic pursuits; or a more fashionable way to express this is that groups broaden the sphere of the political.

So why does organized participation neither boom nor diminish significantly following re-democratization? The key is that organizations can be very flexible entities when their survival is at stake (March 1982). Upon observing environmental changes, organizations respond accordingly. Such a reaction may necessitate dramatic changes in the organization, its membership, or its goals. Therefore, if organizations react to the changes wrought by democratization — the opening of political space, more competition, new rules, the emergence of the electoral realm — they can adjust their behavior and expectations in order to ride out the waves of uncertainty and transition.

A TRANSFORMED CIVIL SOCIETY

My research indicates that most organizations undergo a process of transformation in response to such a change in their political environment. By way of illustration, I have adapted and updated Oxhorn's table (1992: 379) depicting the dynamics of organizational transformation to demonstrate how groups respond to a transition to democracy (see Table 7.1). As shown in Chapter 5, organizations become more localized in response to the municipalization process, a lack of funding on the national level, and the fragmentation of social movements. In order to obtain funding from the decreasing universe of available sources, groups broaden their scope of activities so that they can "sell" themselves under various categories. Organizations become much more particularistic in part because after having focused on the collective "good" in fighting the dictatorship for so long, individuals seek to fulfill their own needs. Finally, groups adapt to the change in political environment by de-politicizing, as demonstrated by the cases in Chapter 4. De-politicization occurs first because much of the funding destined for civil society dries up after a democratic regime consolidates, and groups must become self-sufficient in order to survive. Second, many groups achieve their primary goal with the end of the dictatorship; it often proves difficult for them to agree upon another mission, particularly one which all of their members can agree upon with enthusiasm. Finally, as already noted above, organizations may become less overtly political as a reaction to their disappointment or disillusionment with the spoils (or lack thereof) of democracy.[4]

Table 7.1
THE TRANSFORMATION OF ORGANIZATIONS
UNDER RE-DEMOCRATIZATION*

	PRIOR DEMOCRATIC REGIME (Through 1973)	AUTHORITARIAN REGIME (1973-1990)	NEW DEMOCRATIC REGIME (1990-present)
Level of Organizational Focus	Local & national level	National level	Local level
Target of Organizations	Particularistic	Universalistic	Particularistic
Politicization of Organizations	Focus on state, especially executive branch. (Growing levels of politicization, 1970-73)	Highly politicized; focus on regime type & repression; every-thing takes on political symbolism.	Focus on power relationships in community, family & personal life.
Nature of Social Movements	Lack of collective identity in civil society. (Only labor movement is strong)	(In the 1980s) Many strong & interconnected movements: labor, women, human rights. High level of collective identity.	Fragmented movements, organizations atomized. Lack of collective identity.
Relationships Between Organizations and External Actors	Organizations dependent on political parties. (State corporatism through "Promoción Popular" program)	Parties take backseat to social movements; most organizations are autonomous from parties. Organizations largely excluded from state realm. (Growing state corporatism in the 1980s)	Parties reemerge to dominate national politics; limited autonomy for organizations on a local level. Formal institutional channels established in state, but little contact between organizations and the state on the national level, except for funding.

* Information specific to the Chilean case is noted in italics within parentheses.

The Chilean case study illustrates that after re-democratization, the transformed organizations constitute a civil society that is diffuse throughout and dense at the lower levels. Organized participation is dense at the lower levels and destitute at the upper tiers because of the fragmentation of social movements and umbrella groups, rendering organizations atomized, locally-focused and often incommunicative due to the lack of a hierarchy or coordinating body. The word which best depicts contemporary civil society is *frustum* — it is like a cone or pyramid which was densely populated at all levels, but following the return to democracy the top third of it was lopped off as national hierarchies disbanded and movements disappeared. In the case of Chilean civil society, the "top" which disappeared was spearheaded by the Vicaría, the Cruzada, the labor movement and the women's movement. As opposed to under the prior democratic regime, organizations in Chile have maintained their autonomy from political parties and the state. Instead of reaching out and organizing factions within civil society, the government has created state agencies which officially represent the interests of different sectors of the population.[3] Political parties, although regaining much of their power and membership base, have limited much of their organizing to the electoral realm leaving social groups largely untouched. With the dissolution of the Vicaría, civil society groups are much less dependent on the Catholic Church now than during the authoritarian regime. Therefore, organizations have sustained their autonomous position vis-a-vis the institutions which have historically dominated Chilean civil society. Many participants claim to have "learned from history," and insist that they will not allow their organizations to be controlled by political parties nor will they allow them to pressure the state with too many demands as occurred in the early 1970s under Allende. Some fear a return to the military dictatorship, others are apprehensive of a reversion to socialism.

This is illustrative of how organizational and individual memories have been critical to this argument; such "memory banks" are possible only because Chile is a case of re-democratization. The fact is that all citizens (and organizations) over the age of thirty-five at the time the military regime left office in 1990 could conceivably recall and either reproduce or reject their participatory routines, behaviors, linkages and sentiments from the prior democratic regime of the 1960s. Therefore, it is likely that since this is a case of a return to democracy, it is easier for organizations to adjust their behavior and expectations to participating under democratic rules. Second time democratic contenders such as Argentina, Chile and Venezuela thus presumably have civil societies which are better equipped than those undergoing a first-time democratization to transform to meet the changes wrought by the emerging democracy, and are better prepared to know which actions to bypass so as to avoid de-railing the democracy. Could organizations, in El Salvador or Haiti for example, react in a similar fashion without the benefit of a prior democratic experience? A quick glance at those countries would yield civil societies that are struggling to define a role amidst emerging political party systems and increased societal violence.

THE OTHER PATHS

Having discussed the path of transformation and its predominance within civil society following re-democratization, what of the other three potential paths which I had hypothesized — continuation, de-mobilization, or incorporation? My research indicates that there are few generalizable types of organizations that follow those paths; only isolated cases of individual organizations emerge within each trajectory. For example, the self-help housing organizations that started throughout Chile in the late 1980s have continued mobilizing with an increased number of participants. Because their activities are largely within the economic realm and narrowly focussed, the transition back to democracy had little effect on their goals and foci. They are an instance of the path of "continuation."[6] Surprisingly, despite the strength of both the Chilean state and political parties, I found no examples of organizations which followed the path of "incorporation." Upon beginning my research, I had imagined that human rights groups would be the most likely to incorporate into other institutions. Human rights groups were formed en masse in the 1970s and 1980s in response to the abuses of the dictatorship, spearheading the fight against the Pinochet

regime. Once those rights were again protected, it would seem logical for those organizations to merge either with a political party or
the state. Since the human rights leaders largely guided the anti-
authoritarian movement, it was expected that they would work for
the new institutions for which they had fought so hard; without
their strong and experienced leaders, many groups either disband
or follow the leader, merging with the new institution. In fact, I
could not find any examples of human rights groups that had
undergone such an incorporation, although there are a few such
groups, like the Vicaría, which have disbanded or mutated[7].
There are, however, instances in which an organization has ceased to exist
after its leader left to work for the government.[8] Of these three trajectories, it is the path of de-mobilization which encompasses
more of the outliers. Most notably, as discussed in Chapter 6, poor
strategy choices coupled with exogenous factors such as the
Catholic Church, funding constraints, and the state's SERNAM
(National Service for Women) have led the feminist movement and
women's identity groups to disband.

Why do we not find more cases of organizations following the
paths of incorporation, de-mobilization, and especially continuation? These paths are under-represented because a transition
(back) to democracy scrambles many of the expected routines and
rules of society leaving few organizations unaffected; organizations
may be forced into a situation in which they must respond to those
changes or die (disband). For example, a transition may affect
opportunities for participation, channels of representation, availability of funding, and the social hierarchy. In other words,
(re)democratization changes the environment in more ways than
the one Huntington predicts (opening opportunities for mobilization which leads to more interaction with the state). Instead, re-
democratization affects the funding possibilities, the attitudes of
members, the space for effective action focused on the state, and
the number of organizations competing for members. Therefore,
any organization which has activities or goals connected to the
political or social realms is likely to feel the effect of (re)democra-
tization. The groups' goals may have been attained, their funding
may have dried up, their leaders may have abandoned the group to
work for the government. Few groups are insulated from the reper-

cussions of a transition to democracy. If organizations are to survive, they must adapt to the changes in the political environment
which threaten their existence; most groups thus follow the path of
transformation, or to a much lesser extent, demobilization.

RESEARCHING PARTICIPATION AND DEMOCRATIZATION

A word of caution about the universality of this research. It is
important to note the particularities of the Chilean political system
— re-democratization, much past state involvement in civil society, strong party tradition, historically powerful Church role — and
to question whether the answers given herein are generalizable.
The peculiarities of the Chilean case would play an important role
in identifying comparable cases for future study; no other Latin
American country boasts the same combination of political factors.
Venezuela lacks the strong Church presence, Brazil has never had
the same high level of political party organizing, Uruguay's party
system lacks the strength and three-way split between the left, center and right. One should also consider whether and how the
length of the transition affects the transformative capabilities of
civil society. Does a short transition, like in the case of Argentina,
impede adaptation of organizations? Munck (in Foweraker and
Craig, 1990: 31-2) suggests that civil society is less likely to demobilize during a long transition because organizations have time to
observe changing trends and adapt accordingly. On the other hand,
longer transitions can also mean too much time in "limbo" — time
when organizations are unsure of the rules, behavioral norms, and
funding sources. Although such lengthy periods of uncertainty may
be seen as posing an obstacle for civil society, Chile is an example
of a long transition, and as evidenced by the preceding chapters, its
civil society has been able to transform successfully.

I have two observations to make about doing research on participation levels. First, it is important to stress that those studying
civil society must rethink their measures of organizational success
and failure. As an environment changes, so too should the signals
of success; just as environments are not static, measures of organizational progress cannot be static. The definitions of success

should be flexible. Organizations should not be assessed solely according to longevity or consistency, nor should they primarily be judged in the short-run. The most difficult task is not for organizations to adapt, but for those of us outside their arena to recognize this adaptation. Second, scholars should make a better attempt to measure the intensity rather than just the level of organized participation, a challenge which I have tried to overcome with limited success.[9] For an even richer study and a deeper understanding of how civil societies transform after democratization and the types of democracy which subsequently emerge, a study would need time-series projects that assess changes in the following: the time citizens spend participating per week, the priority each individual gives to involvement in civil society, and the citizens' expressed commitment to different types of organization.

There are, of course, innumerable factors which are to be taken into account when defining the type of a democratic regime, of which organized group participation is just one. Although this book has established that civil society persists following a transition to democracy, I do not mean to imply that the Chilean case is a partici)atory democracy. As evidenced by the previous chapter on women's organizing, it is questionable whether the right to participation is accessible and exercised by all groups of citizens after re-democratization. As groups become less political and more localized, they leave behind (and unoccupied) much public space — space which originally served organizations well under the dictatorship now becomes repossessed by the state and political parties. Therefore, although civil society may be more participatory overall than during the authoritarian regime, the contemporary democracy may be less participatory and representative than many had hoped it would be.[10] These expectations often result in the disillusionment of the citizenry with an emerging democracy. In order to deal with such disillusionment as well as with the other by-products of democratization, organizations must transform or confront the prospect of de-mobilization. Those that transform successfully can ultimately play an important role, be it positive or negative, in the consolidation of the democracy.

THE IMPLICATIONS OF A TRANSFORMED
CIVIL SOCIETY

This study has established that organizations and institutions react
to and are affected by changes in their political environment. But
organizations are not only reactive, but also pro-active entities;
they can and do affect their environments.[11] Having discussed the
effect of (re-) democratization on civil society, we can now reverse
the variables by asking, how does the transformed civil society
affect and facilitate the stability of an emerging democracy? How
also does it affect the quality of the participation in the democratic regime?[12] There are six ways in which a transformed civil society
may bode well for democracy.

First, many of the transformed organizations *serve as "nurseries" of
democracy*. They essentially function as schools in which citizens can
learn how to vote and make consensual decisions. In larger organizations, members discover the importance of having a "voice" or
representation in the decision-making processes which affect their
lives. Leaders also master the techniques of campaigning, fostering dialogue, and delegating responsibility; such activities within
an organization cultivate democratic culture and values in citizens.
Organizations also impart more general skills useful in a myriad of
political, economic and social situations. Participants may learn to
debate and dialogue, express opinions clearly, organize events,
lead and record meetings, promote positive group dynamics, be
involved in decision-making processes, and be flexible in the face
of change or adversity. By teaching citizens (and giving them a
space in which to practice) the skills and techniques necessary for
them to play an active and informed role in a democracy, organizations contribute to the stability and quality of the regime.[13]

Second, participation in organizations *fosters active citizenship and
provides "ownership" of the democracy to citizens*. By becoming involved
in civil society groups, participants acquire a stake in the political
system. If citizens feel that the democracy is "theirs", they will
connect their success to the regime's success. Similarly, the key
is that citizens feel as though the stability of their social system is
linked to the stability of the regime. If they can claim a significant

stake in the system, they are likely to be more concerned about it and more motivated to protect their common interests. For many organizations and members, supporting the new democratic regime has meant moderating their demands and expectations — for the good of the regime and for their own good. Some, like Huntington (1968), have argued that if citizens push too hard they may compromise the stability of the regime, and in doing so, may end up with a system that is less "participant-friendly." The more that citizens participate in aspects of the democratic system, the more they will value democracy as a regime type and will struggle to uphold it.[14] Organizations can also provide ownership of a "civilized" system to some "un-civil" citizens; civil society organizations can furnish new loyalties for those who may potentially be dangerous to democracy, such as disgruntled military personnel or ex-combatants.[15]

Parallel to this, is that an organized civil society focused on local issues and problems may help manage social conflict. Valenzuela argues that in order to facilitate the consolidation of democracy, a society must have frameworks for channeling and resolving social conflict (1990: 28-30). He suggests that the key is the creation of adequate "social demand processing settlements," which may include the: creation of state institutions; establishment of organizations (with leaders who can direct them); development of agreed upon procedures to resolve conflict between organized groups; and the existence of links between civil society and the legislature/executive to ensure parallel consensus processes. These social demand settlements are said to be most helpful in facilitating democratic consolidation when they operate with a minimum of politicization — a condition to which we already know the newly transformed civil societies adhere.

Third, many of the transformed organizations, or interest associations, *provide for the needs* (particularly economic) *of the citizenry*. They teach skills which are useful to their members in the household and economic sectors, such as accounting, public-speaking, sewing, cooking, or child-rearing. At times, the groups act as cooperatives with members jointly providing services (like child-care or senior citizen-care) that each participant could not afford individually. Some organizations also sponsor revenue projects which supplement household food and income levels. Others act as incubators of development by re-distributing goods, providing alternative income sources, and finding local and immediate solutions to the economic problems of citizens.[16] By doing so, civil society contributes to the stability of the democracy by alleviating the demands placed on the state to meet those needs. The more satisfied citizens are with their lives (as well as their role in the society), the less likely they will be to de-rail the political system.

Fourth, participation in organizations also *builds individual and group identity, and nurtures a sense of community.* Networks, contacts, and friendships are fostered through participation, which leads to increased sharing of information and ideas. Those involved in civil society groups often report a boost in their level of self-confidence, as they become accustomed to interacting and expressing opinions around individuals outside of their immediate circle. Valdés et. al. (1993: 108) cite a *pobladora* from Puente Alto on the confidence-building value of participating in social organizations, *"y que uno va teniendo más personalidad para decir las cosas, porque me ponía harto nerviosa."*[17] In addition to boosting their self-confidence, participation allows individuals to explore and exercise the different facets of their multiple identities. For example, a women might identify herself as a church-goer, unionist, and mother all at once and have opportunities to participate in organizations related to each facet of her idenity.[18]

Fifth, the transformed organizations *ferry democracy to a deeper and wider audience.* By becoming more localized, groups bring democracy and democratic decisions to the neighborhoods where the process appears more intimate. They also attract different people to participate who might not have been involved in the realm of national social movement organizing during the authoritarian phase. By transporting democracy to a more personal and local level, civil society organizations heighten the quality of democracy. Closely related is the final way in which a transformed civil society bodes well for democracy: the organizations which have transformed and therefore, have successfully avoided being co-opted by the state or subsumed under a political party, may *represent a venue for the expression of alternative political viewpoints.* As some citizens may feel unable or unwilling to express opposition to government leaders and policies or to voice their radical political beliefs through official channels, civil society provides what may be seen as a safer or more responsive route through which they can be activists. If these transformed organizations can contribute positively to their environment, there are also ways in which they can negatively effect that same environment, or in this case, may detract from the stability and quality of the emerging democracy. First, the manner in which civil society has transformed *leaves few opportunities or channels for representation of citizens' interests* to the state. The de-politicization factor means that as most organizations shy away from the political realm, citizens have little recourse for input into policy-making; their needs and demands may not be represented in the decision-making process. As long as citizens remain satisfied with their lives and their perception of state progress, and as long as civil society organizations are able to continue to provide for their needs, then this is not problematic. However, the stability of the democracy may be endangered in the long-run if a deep crisis, economic or otherwise, draws citizens' attention to the deficiencies of the decision-making process without simultaneously offering solutions to fix those defects. This problem is further magnified by the fact that of the input which leaders do receive from non-state actors, it is heavily weighted toward political parties. As organizations withdraw from the national level, they concede much national policy influence to the parties, which in the Chilean case, are traditionally not representative of large sectors of society — particularly women and minorities. The transformation of civil society after a return to democracy assures that these new regimes do not end up with a citizen-less democracy or spectator democracy. It does, however, mean these countries are more likely to *end up with a gendered, or in this case a "masculine", democracy — in other words, the disbanding of women's organizations may leave the newly emerging democracies with few women's voices and few channels to represent the diversity of women's needs and ideas.*

Second, without the pressures and demands for accountability from so many lobbying groups and citizens-watch organizations, elected officials and government bureaucrats may be able to complete their work more quickly and efficiently. However, while the de-politicization of organizations may *lead bureaucratic decision-making to be more productive and rapid*, the inverse of this is that the de-politi-cization of organizations *leads to the existence of few checks and balances on state power.* Therefore, the state can more easily be captured by a single interest group. It endangers the stability and quality of the democracy if there are no non-governmental watchdogs of state action and policy. The danger of this is enshrined in the slogan of KABATID, a pro-democracy women's organization in the Philippines, which states that "We get the government we demand and deserve" (in Diamond, 1992).

Third, the localization of civil society groups *allows for little coordi-nation and sharing of ideas and information* between organizations them-selves, as well as between organizations and the state. The frag-mentation of movements and umbrella groups has minimized interactions within civil society, bringing idea development and information exchange to a minimum. The less interchange of this sort, the more ineffectual and superficial decision-making process-es will be, both internal and external to the state.

Fourth, *particularism may encourage excessive individualism or isolation of individuals and groups,* which can only work against efforts to build community and to ensure the rights of groups. Fifth, the *economiza-tion of organizations can be a dangerous phenomenon.* It may breed a gen-eration which believes that participation is only worthwhile if it brings economic benefits as well. In other words, it may engender a society which views the principles of a particular political system — in this case, democracy — as an insufficient measure of the value or success of that system.

Finally, the transformation of civil society is, at its root, about *bypassing the state,* which may alternately be viewed as a positive or negative by-product. As organizations become both more localized and more adept at forging transnational linkages, the state may be seen as being "out of the loop." The state may then enjoy less legit-imacy domestically and internationally. There are, therefore, both positive and negative effects of organizational transformation on the quality and stability of democracy.

In democratization, causation and change run in both directions. There are, in fact, two parallel processes of consolidation going on in these countries in political transition — a consolidation of a regime and another consolidation of civil society. These processes of consolidation are somewhat akin to bike riding, where the "lead" may be passed from one to another and then back again — as each takes turns riding in the easier tail-winds of the other; this helps both to finish. With less balance, or by choosing to go it alone, neither may complete the ride.

Organized participation has outlived re-democratization. Levels of group participation after the transition have been neither startlingly successful nor a radical failure. Organizations in Latin America, and in Chile in particular, have transformed to adapt to their new political environment by becoming more local and particularistic, as well as less overtly political than during the authoritarian era. Salvador Allende was correct when he predicted that the *grandes alamedas* would once again be opened; but in the end, the levels, arenas and foci of the peoples' participation on those *alamedas* look very different than he and many scholars had ever imagined. The short-term implications of this transformed civil society are promising for the stability of the regimes, but call into question the longer-term quality of the emerging democracies.

Notes

1. Robert Michels (1962: 338).

2. Translated: "Politics in Latin America is defined more in terms of participation — or non-participation — than in terms of representation" (Alain Tourraine, 1988: 137).

3. Huntington's argument actually refers to that which happens to participation once democratic rule has been fully consolidated. Readers may rightly note that Chile's democracy is not yet fully consolidated as the military still enjoys some autonomy and political power. Yet as democratization deepens in Chile, participation patterns do appear to be unfolding in a manner distinct from that which Huntington hypothesized.

4. At this point, it may be important to remind the reader that by using the term "de-politicization," I am not claiming that the transformed

organizations are not political in nature. Rather, using a narrow definition of the "political," they cease to focus on that which is related to the policies and institutions of the state or regime; this is particularly the case at the national level, and much less applicable at the municipal level. This does not mean that these organizations are no longer concerned with relationships of power in society — be it in firms, other organizations, the family or the personal realm. Such relationships do exist in post-transition civil society, and I consider them to be highly "political" in content. I could have defined "de-politicization" to mean "expansion of the realm of the political" in order to encompass the notion that organizations are now approaching neighborhoods, schools, and households as being highly "political" arenas. However, I have retained the terminology employed in the literature on civil society and democratization. A broad definition of "political" would have been more commensurate with the terms and debates in the literature on feminism and the women's movement. See Kirkwood (1986), and Chapter 6 of this book.

  5.   Examples are the National Service for Women (SERNAM) and the National Institute for Youth (INJ).

  6.   Leonardo Moreno Nuñez, Chief of Staff for the Ministry of Housing, interview with the author on August 13, 1992. See Blom (1994) for more on women's self-help housing organizations in Santiago.

  7.   Raúl Rettig, president of Chile's Commission on Truth and Reconciliation, expressed his belief that "there is and might always be a role for human rights organizations in Chile, whether they treat the rights of all, of women, or of ethnics." He argues that the human rights groups of the 1980s have not been incorporated by the state, it just solicits their opinion more than was the case under the dictatorship. In interview with the author on August 11, 1992.

  8.   I cannot prove that these organizations have disbanded because their leaders left; however, chronologically, the leaders first incorporated into the state agencies, and sometime later, the organizations ceased to function. In interviews with members of now-defunct organizations, individuals consistently cited their leaders departure as an important factor contributing to lowered enthusiasm and loyalty of the members, which they argued, triggered an eventual disbanding of the organization. One could argue that this was the case for the Vicaría.

  9.   There is a pronounced absence of this type of information available; I have found no polls recording such data in a time-series fashion.

Surveys done by PET and CEP are just now being published which include these questions. The contemporary period thus becomes the Time 1 for such data on the intensity of participation. The other solution would have been for the researcher (me) to have administered such surveys to the subject organizations and members in the late 1980s and then again around 1994. Unfortunately, I was not conducting research on this subject in the late 1980s, and have found no other researcher who systematically focused on such questions during that period.

10.   It is my impression that civil society is at least as participatory or more so now than under the prior democratic regime in Chile; however, this study lacks the time series data to prove this assertion.

11.   See March and Olsen (1989: 162) and March (1988: 176). Hannan and Freeman (1989) similarly argue that environments affect and are affected by organizations. They posit that societies with few forms of organizations have difficulty responding to environmental changes (1989: 8).

12.   Herein, "stability" is defined in terms of the resilience and persistence of the regime type. "Quality" is defined as the depth and breadth of democratic participation —how many citizens, from how many sectors of society are participating. On the broader topic of the quality of democracy, we would have to look at the universe of institutions, not just civil society. Note that the questions are particular to how a transformed civil society (as defined in this study) affects democratic consolidation. For a more general, theoretical overview of how participation effects democracy, see the collection of essays in Diamond (1992), particularly those by Diamond, Pascual, and Zavala. See also Schmitter (1993b).

13.   On organizations as nurseries of democracy, see Schmitter (1993b). It is important to note that not all organizations within a democracy function in an internally democratic manner.

14.   As Patricio Frías (1992: 25) notes in the case of labor organizing, "one is able to see an important level of maturity, responsibility, and moderation of unionism in its demands and mobilizations, because of its commitment to a democratic government, and its willingness to protect the transition process." For more thoughts on this theme of protection of the democracy by citizens, see Valenzuela (1990: 13). While some may consider this "protection" of democracy, others are likely to see it as being "co-opted" or "tamed" by the government.

Another way to look at this issue is that participating in organizations may lead to the development of citizenship and citizen satisfaction. Group participation is important because it allows people to activate their citizenship. Active citizenship can be seen as that which is taken by oneself — through participating, mobilizing oneself, speaking out on an issue. Conversely, passive citizenship may be viewed as that which is given, by the state — formal rights in the form of laws and norms. Active citizenship likely leads to higher levels of loyalty to the political system, and the belief by citizens that it is a collective good for which they are responsible. A localized civil society can therefore lead to active citizenship and a deeper and more stable democracy because citizens feel as though the political system "belongs" to them. On these issues related to citizenship and democracy, see Schild (1992) and Schmitter (1993b).

15.   I am grateful to Harold Trinkunas for this insight.

16.   As Winnie Lira, Director of the Fundación Solidaridad, said to me, "These organizations are a type of small development — an incubator of development at the local level." In interview with the author on August 2, 1994.

17.   Translation: "and one begins to have more personality about saying things, because I used to get very nervous." With regard to community, I very much like the Filipino expression, "bayanihan." According to Filipino civil society activist Dette Pascual, "bayanihan" is the ancient Filipino spirit of community. In current usage, it refers to any action calling for the participation and unity of the community (in Diamond, 1992: 69).

18.   For more on multiple facets of an individual's identity, see Schild (1992), Melucci (1980), and Touraine (1989).

Founding versus Legal Status of Functional Organizations[1]

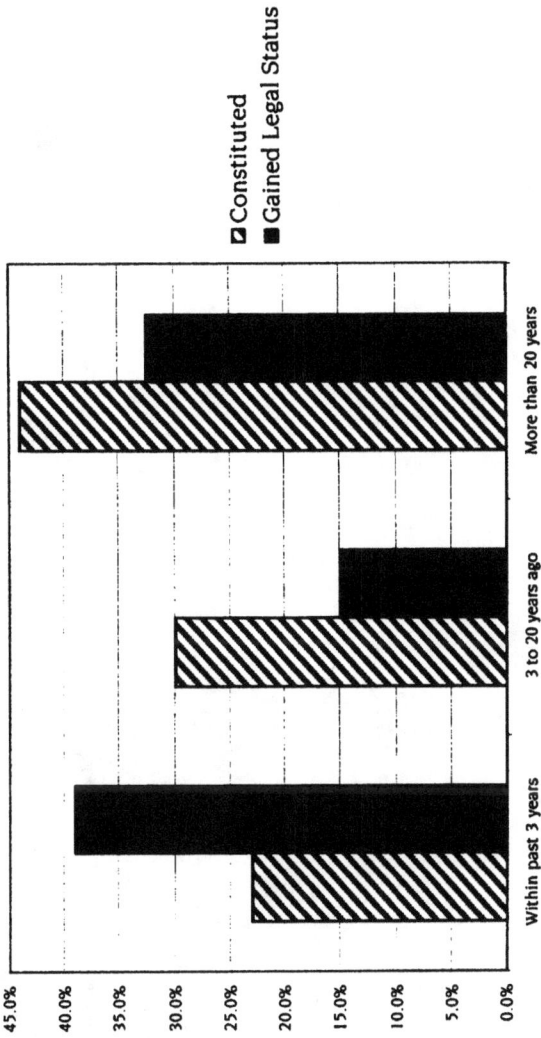

Legend:
- Constituted
- Gained Legal Status

Categories: Within past 3 years, 3 to 20 years ago, More than 20 years

Axis: 0.0%, 5.0%, 10.0%, 15.0%, 20.0%, 25.0%, 30.0%, 35.0%, 40.0%, 45.0%

¹Source: CENPROS, "Encuesta participación y organización social." Santiago, Chile. May 1994.

Founding versus Legal Status of Territorial Organizations[1]

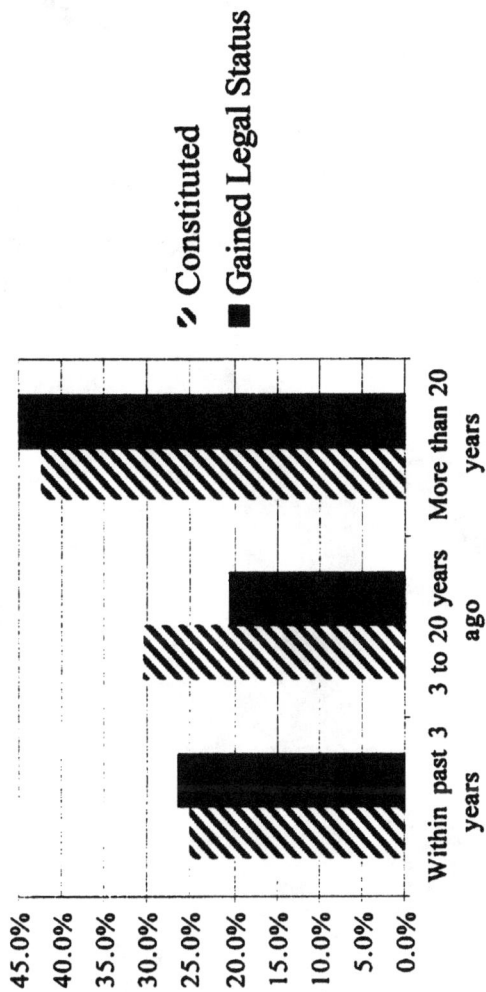

Legend:
- Constituted
- Gained Legal Status

Categories:
- Within past 3 years
- 3 to 20 years ago
- More than 20 years

Values axis: 0.0%, 5.0%, 10.0%, 15.0%, 20.0%, 25.0%, 30.0%, 35.0%, 40.0%, 45.0%

Source: CENPROS, "Encuesta participación y organización social." Santiago, Chile. May 1994.

Select Bibiliography

Agüero, Felipe and Jeffrey Stark (eds.). 1998. *Fault Lines of Democracy in Post-Transition Latin America.* University of Miami: North-South Center Press.

Alburquerque, Mario. 1993. "Una reflexión sobre la relación entre actores sociales y democracia." *Economía & Trabajo.* Año I, no. 2. Santiago, Chile: PET. Pp. 5-24.

Alburquerque, Mario and Victor Zúñiga. 1987. "Democracia, participación y unidad." Santiago: CEDAL.

Aldrich, Howard E. 1979. *Organizations and Environments.* Englewood Cliffs, New Jersey: Prentice Hall.

Allan, Pamela, Margarita Fernandez, and Roberto Urmeneta. 1991. "Las organizaciones economicas populares de consumo, 1989-1991." Cartilla de Capacitacion y Difusion No. 49. Santiago: PET.

Angell, Alan. 1970. *Partidos políticos y movimiento obrero en Chile.* Mexico City: UNAM.

Alvarez, Sonia. 1990. *Engendering Democracy in Brazil.* Princeton: Princeton University Press.

Arteaga, Ana Maria. 1988. "Politización de la privado y subversión de lo cotidiano." *Mundo de Mujer.* Santiago: Centro de Estudios de la Mujer.

Barnes, Samuel, Max Kaase, et al. 1979. *Political Action: Mass Participation in Five Western Democracies.* Beverly Hills: Sage Press.

Barrera, Manuel and Gonzalo Falabella (eds.). 1989. *Sindicatos bajo regimenes militares.* Santiago: United Nations Research Institute for Social Development.

Bendix, Reinhard. 1990. "State and Civil Society in Modern Western Democracies." Unpublished manuscript.

Bentham, Jeremy. 1882. *Theory of Legislation*. London: Trubner Press.

Berger, Suzanne (ed.). 1981. *Organizing Interests in Western Europe*. London: Cambridge University Press.

Borja, Jordi, et al. 1989. *Decentralización y Democracia*. Santiago, Chile: SUR.

_____. 1987. *Decentralización del Estado: Movimiento Social y Gestion Local*. Santiago, Chile: FLACSO.

Boschi, Renato. 1984. "On Social Movements and Democratization: Theoretical Issues." Stanford/Berkeley Occasional Papers in Latin American Studies.

Bourque, Susan C. 1989. "Gender and the State: Perspectives from Latin America," in Sue Ellen Charlton et. al. (eds.), *Women, the State, and Development*. Albany: State University of New York Press.

Brand, Karl-Werner. 1990. "Cyclical Aspects of New Social Movements," in Russell Dalton and Manfred Kuechler (eds.), *Challenging the Political Order*. Oxford: Oxford University Press. Pp. 23-42.

Brysk, Alison. 1994. *The Politics of Human Rights in Argentina: Protest, Change, and Democratization*. Stanford: Stanford University Press.

Bunster-Burotto, Ximena. 1988. "Watch Out for the Little Nazi Man That All of Us Have Inside: The Mobilization and Demobilization of Women in Militarized Chile." *Women's Studies International Forum* 11, no. 5. Summer. Pp. 485-91.

Burnett, Ben G. 1970. *Political Groups in Chile: The Dialogue Between Order and Change*. Austin: University of Texas Press.

Campero, Guillermo. 1987. *Entre la sobrevivencia y la acción política: Las organizaciones de pobladores en Santiago*. Santiago, Chile: ILET.

_____. 1993. "Sindicalismo en los '90: desafíos y perspectivas." *Economía & Trabajo*. Año I, no. 2. PET: Santiago, Chile. Pp. 25-44.

Campero, G. and R. Cortazar. 1988. "Actores sociales y la transición a la democracia en Chile." Colección Estudios CIEPLAN. No. 25., December. Pp. 115-158.

Cañadell, Rosa M. 1993. "Chilean Women's Organizations: Their Potential for Change." *Latin American Perspectives*. Issue 79, vol. 20, no. 4, fall. Pp. 43-60.

Carrion, F. et al. 1991. *Municipio y Democracia*. Santiago, Chile: SUR.

Carroll, Glen R. 1984. "Organizational Ecology." *Annual Review of Sociology*. Pp. 71-93.

Cavarozzi, Marcelo and Vicente Palermo. 1993. "State, Civil Society, and Popular Neighborhood Organizations in Argentina's Transition to Democracy." Unpublished manuscript.

Centro de Estudios y Promoción Social (CENPROS). 1994. "Encuesta participación y organización social en 14 comunas de Chile, 1993." Santiago, Chile: CENPROS.

Centros de Estudios Públicos. 1987-1993. "Estudio Social y de Opinion Pública." Documentos de Trabajo. Santiago, Chile: CEP.

Chaney, Elsa. 1974. "The Mobilization of Women in Allende's Chile," in Jane Jaquette (ed.), Women in Politics. New York: John Wiley & Sons. Pp. 267-279.

Charlín, Marcelo and Sergio Rojas. 1992. "Participación, Concertación y Partenariado, la descentalización del Estado en una perspective local: ideas para un discusión." Documento de Trabajo. Santiago, Chile: FLACSO.

Ciorino, Rossana and Montse Moreto. 1992. "Intentando Nacer de Nuevo." Santiago, Chile: Ediciones LOM.

CLACSO workshop. 1990. Movimientos Sociales y Política: el desafio de la democracia en America Latina. Santiago, Chile: CES.

Cohen, Jean. 1985. "Strategy or Identity: New Theoretical Paradigms and Contemporary Social Movements." Social Research. Vol. 52, no. 4. Pp. 663-716.

Colburn, Forrest D. (ed.). 1990. Prospects for Democracy in Latin America. Monograph Series, No. 1. Princeton: Center for International Studies.

Comisión Económica para América Latina. CEPAL. 1992. Equidad y Transformación Productiva: un enfoque integrado. Santiago, Chile: CEPAL.

Crummett, Maria de los Angeles. 1977. "El Poder Femenino: The Mobilization of Women Against Socialism in Chile." Latin American Perspectives. Vol. 4, no. 4. Pp. 103-113.

CUT. 1993. "Propuesta de la CUT a los Candidatos Presidenciales." Informativo Unidad y Trabajo, No. 37. Santiago, Chile: CUT.

_____. 1991. "Plan de Trabajo de la CUT." First National Congress of the CUT. In Informativo CUT: Unidad y Trabajo, No. 17. Santiago, Chile: CUT.

_____. 1989. "Propuesta para la Transición a la Democracia." Santiago, Chile: CUT.

Dahl, Robert. 1982. Dilemmas of Pluralist Democracy. New Haven: Yale University Press.

_____. 1971. *Polyarchy: Participation and Opposition*. New Haven: Yale University Press.

de Toqueville, Alexis. 1832/1956. *Democracy in America*. New York: Penguin Books.

Diamond, Irene (ed.). 1983. *Families, Politics, and Public Policies: A Feminist Dialogue on Women and the State*. New York: Longman.

Diamond, Larry. 1992. *The Democratic Revolution*. New York: Freedom House.Dore, Elizabeth (ed.). 1997. *Gender Politics in Latin America: Debates in Theory and Practice*. New York: Monthly Review Press.

Drake, Paul and Ivan Jaksic (eds.). 1991. *The Struggle for Democracy in Chile, 1982-1990*. Lincoln: University of Nebraska Press.

Echeverría Bascuñán, Fernando and Jorge Rojas Hernández (eds.). 1992. *Añoranzas, Sueños, Realidades: dirigents sindicales hablan de la transición*. Santiago, Chile: Ediciones SUR.

Eckstein, Susan (ed.). 1989. *Power and Popular Protest: Latin American Social Movements*. Berkeley: University of California Press.

Escobar, Arturo and Sonia Alvarez, (eds.) 1992. *The Making of Social Movements in Latin America: Identity, Strategy and Democracy*. Boulder: Westview Press.

Evers, Tilman. 1985. "Identity: The Hidden Sides of New Social Movements in Latin America," In David Slater (ed.), *New Social Movements and the State in Latin America*. The Netherlands: Foris Publications.

Fernandez, Margarita et. al. 1994. "Participación Comunitaria en Programas Alimentarios. Programa de Colaciones a Niños y Ancianos a través de Ollas Comunes." Santiago, Chile: PET-PROSAN.

Foweraker, Joe and Ann L. Craig. 1990. *Popular Movements and Political Change in Mexico*. Boulder, Colorado: Lynne Rienner Publishers.

Foxley, Alejandro. 1993. *Economía Política de la Transición*. Santiago: Ediciones Dolmen.

Fitzsimmons, Tracy. 2000 "A Monstrous Regime-nt of Women? State, Regime, and Women's Political Organizing in Latin America." *Latin American Research Review*. Vol. 35, no. 2.

Fitzsimmons, Tracy and Mark Anner. 1999 "Civil Society in a Postwar Period: Labor in the Salvadoran Democratic Transition." *Latin American Research Review*. Vol. 34, no. 3.

Friedman, Elisabeth J. 1998. "Paradoxes of Gendered Political Opportunity in the Venezuelan Transition to Democracy." *Latin American Research Review.* Vol. 33, no. 3. Pp.87-135.

Friedman, John. 1989. "The Latin American Barrio Movement as a Social Movement: Contribution to a Debate." *International Journal of Urban and Regional Research.* Vol. 13, no. 3. Pp. 501-510.

Frías, Patricio. 1994. "La afiliación sindical en Chile: 1932-1992." *Economía & Trabajo.* Año I, no. 2. Santiago, Chile: PET. Pp. 261-290.

———. 1993a. *Construcción del sindicalismo chileno como actor nacional.* Santiago, Chile: PET and CUT.

———. 1993b. "Perspectivas de Renovación Sindical." *Economía y Trabajo en Chile.* Annual Report, 1990-1991. Santiago, Chile: PET.

Frías, Patricio and Jaime Ruiz-Tagle. 1992. "Situación y dinámica del sindicalismo chileno en el contexto económico y sociopolítico." Documento de Trabajo no. 91. Santiago, Chile: PET.

Fundación Solidaridad. 1993-1994. "Memoria Anual." Santiago, Chile.

Gamson, William. 1988. "Political Discourse and Collective Action," in Bert Klandermans, Hanspeter Kriesi, and Sidney Tarrow (eds.), *From Structure to Action: Comparing Social Movement Research Across Cultures.* International Social Movement Research, Vol. I. Greenwich, CT: JAI. Pp. 219-44.

Garcia, Marcelo. 1993. *Más allá de las fronteras: institucionalidad y política de la cooperación internacional en Chile 1990-1994.* Corporación de Cooperación Internacional: Chile.

Garretón, Manuel Antonio. 1990. "Partidos, transición y democracia en Chile." Documento de Trabajo, No. 443. Santiago, Chile: FLACSO.

———. 1989. "Popular Mobilization and the Military Regime in Chile: The Complexities of the Invisible Transition," in Susan Eckstein (ed.), *Power and Popular Protest.* Berkeley: University of California Press.

Gaviola, Edda. 1994. "8 de marzo: día internacional de la mujer, una fecha para reanudar rebeldías." Unpublished manuscript. Santiago, Chile.

Goldrich, Daniel. 1970. "Political Organization and the Politicization of the Poblador." *Comparative Political Studies.* Vol. 3, no. 2. July. Pp. 176-202.

Gonzalez, Raúl. 1994. "Democracia y desarrollo local en los tiempos de la transición: expectativas, realidades y desafíos." *Economía y Trabajo en Chile.* Santiago, Chile: PET. Pp. 177-198.

Guerra Rodriguez, Carlos. 1993. "Participación ciudadana, conjuntos de acción, transición democrática y sectores populares en Santiago de Chile." Unpublished manuscript. Universidad de Salamanca.

Guerra, Pablo. 1994. "Participación sindical: hacia un nuevo perfil del sindicalizado?" *Economía y Trabajo*. Santiago, Chile: PET. Pp. 75-96.

Gusfield, Joseph R. 1955. "Social Structure and Moral Reform: A Study of the Women's Christian Temperance Union." *The American Journal of Sociology*. Vol. 61, no. 3. November. Pp. 221-232.

Hannan, Michael T. and John Freeman. 1989. *Organizational Ecology*. Cambridge: Harvard University Press.

————. 1977. "The Population Ecology of Organizations." *American Journal of Sociology*. March. Pp. 929-64.

Hardy, Clarissa. 1987. *Organizarse para vivir: Pobreza urbana y organización popular*. Santiago, Chile: PET.

Hecht Oppenheim, Lois. 1998. "Reconstructing Democracy and the Role of Women in Politics in Chile." Paper prepared for LASA Conference, September 24-26, 1998.

Held, David (ed.). 1993. *Prospects for Democracy: North, South, East, West*. Stanford: Stanford University Press.

Hola, Eugenia and Gabriela Pischedda. 1993. *Mujeres, Poder y Política*. Centro de Estudios de la Mujer: Santiago, Chile.

Hsiao, Hsin-Huang Michael. 1992. "The Rise of Social Movements and Civil Protests." *Social Change, Liberalization, and Democratization*.

Human Rights Watch. 1987. *The Vicaria de la Solidaridad in Chile*. New York.

Huntington, Samuel. 1991. *The Third Wave: Democratization in the Late Twentieth Century*. University of Oklahoma Press.

————. 1968. *Political Order in Changing Societies*. New Haven: Yale University Press.

Irarrázaval, Ignacio (ed.). 1993. *Desafíos de la descentralización*. Santiago, Chile: Centro de Estudios Públicos.

Jaquette, Jane S. 1994a. "Los Movimientos de Mujeres y las Transiciones Democráticas en América Latina," in Magdalena León (ed.), *Mujeres y Participación Política Avances y desafíos en América Latina*. Bogota: TM Editores. Pp. 117-139.

————. (ed.). 1994b. *The Women's Movement in Latin America*. Revised second edition. Boulder, Colorado: Westview Press.

————. (ed.). 1989. *The Women's Movement in Latin America*. London: Unwin Hyman.

Jaquette, Jane S. And Sharon L. Wolchik (eds.). 1998. *Women and Democracy: Latin America and Central and Eastern Europe.* Baltimore: The Johns Hopkins University Press.

Jelin, Elizabeth. 1990. *Women and Social Change in Latin America.* London: Zed Books.

Jelin, Elizabeth, and Pablo Azcárate. 1991. "Memoría y Política: movimientos de derechos humanos y construcción democrática." *Revista de Ciencias Sociales.* No. 1. América Latina, Hoy. Pp. 29-38.

Karl, Terry L. 1990. "Dilemmas of Democratization in Latin America." *Comparative Politics.* Vol. 23, no. 1, October. Pp. 1-21.

Karl, Terry L. and Philippe Schmitter. 1991. "Democratization around the Globe: Opportunities and Risks." In Michael T. Klare and Daniel C. Thomas (eds.), *World Security.* New York: St. Martin's Press.

Kirkwood, Julieta. 1986. *Ser política en Chile: Las feministas y los partidos.* Santiago, Chile: FLACSO.

_____. 1981. "Chile: La mujer en la formación política." Documento de Trabajo No. 109. Santiago, Chile: FLACSO.

Landsberger, Henry and Tim McDaniel. 1976. "Hypermobilization in Chile 1970-1973." *World Politics.* Vol. 28, no. 4. July.

Lee, M. M. 1976. "Why Few Women Hold Public Office: Democracy and Sexual Roles." *Political Science Quarterly.* No. 91. Pp. 297-314.

Legassa, Maria Victoria. 1993. "Gobierno Local y Políticas Sociales en el Gran Santiago." Santiago, Chile: PET.

León, Magdalena (ed.). 1994. *Mujeres y Participación Política Avances y desafíos en América Latina.* Bogota: TM Editores.

Levy, Daniel C. 1986. "Chilean Universities under the Junta: Regime and Policy." *Latin American Research Review.* Vol. 21, no. 3. Pp. 95-128.

Levy, Susana (ed). 1992 and 1995. "Chile: Mujeres latinoamericanas en cifras." Santiago, Chile: Instituto de la Mujer y FLACSO.

Maier, Charles (ed.). 1987. *Changing the Boundaries of the Political: Essays on the evolving balance between the state and society, public and private in Europe.* Cambridge: Cambridge University Press.

Mainwaring, Scott. 1987. "Urban Popular Movements, Identity and Democratization in Brazil." *Comparative Political Studies.* Vol. 20, no. 2. July. Pp. 131-59.

March, James G. 1988. *Decisions and Organizations.* Cambridge: Basil Blackwell.

March, James G. and Johan P. Olsen. 1993. "Institutional Perspectives on
Governance." Unpublished manuscript. Stanford University.

March, James G. and Johan P. Olsen. 1989. *Rediscovering Institutions: The
Organizational Basis of Politics.* New York: The Free Press.

Matear, Ann. 1997. "'Desde la protesta a la propuesta': The
Institutionalization of the Women's Movement in Chile," in Elizabeth
Dore (ed.), *Gender Politics in Latin America Debates in Theory and Practice.*
New York: Monthly Review Press. Pp.84-100.

Max-Neef, M. and A. Alizalde. 1989. *Sociedad Civil y Cultura Democrática.*
Santiago, Chile: CEPAUR.

Melucci, Alberto. 1980. "The New Social Movements: A Theoretical
Approach." *Social Science Information.* No. 19. Pp. 199-226.

Messinger, Sheldon. 1955. "Organizational Transformation: A Case Study
of a Declining Social Movement." *American Sociological Review.* Vol. 20.
no. 1. Pp. 3-10.

Michels, Robert. 1962. *Political Parties.* New York: The Free Press.

MIDEPLAN. 1992. "Participación de la Comunidad en el Desarrollo Social.
Logros y Proyecciones." Santiago, Chile: MIDEPLAN.

_____. 1991. "Un proceso de integración al desarrollo: Informe Social
1990-1991." Santiago, Chile: División de Planificación, Estudios e
Inversiones.

Mihovilovic Eterovic, Milenko. 1989. *1000 datos: el trabajador y su organización.*
Editoriales Ariete: Santiago, Chile.

Miller, Robert L., Rick Wilford, and Freda Donoghue. 1999. "Personal
Dynamics as Political Participation." *Political Research Quarterly.* Vol. 52,
no. 2, June. Pp. 269-292.

Molina, Natacha. 1986. *Lo feminino y lo democrático en el Chile de hoy.* Santiago,
Chile: Centro de Estudios y Económicos Sociales.

Morales, Isidro, Guillermo De Los Reyes, and Paul Rich (eds). 1999. *Civil
Society and Democratization.* Thousand Oaks: Sage Publications, Inc. (A
special issue of THE ANNALS of the American Academy of Political
and Social Science, Vol. 565, September 1999.)

Moreno, Leonardo and Camilo Sanchez. 1994. "Ley 18.893 sobre organizaciones comunitarias: alcances y comentarios." Government of
Chile.

Morris, Aldon D. and Carol McClurg Mueller (eds.). 1992. *Frontiers in Social
Movement Theory.* New Haven: Yale University Press.

Moulian, Tomás. 1998. "A Time of Forgetting: The Myths of the Chilean Transition." NACLA. Vol. XXXII, no. 2, September/October. Pp. 16-20.

Munck, Gerardo. 1991. "Social Movements and Democracy in Latin America: Theoretical Debates and Comparative Perspectives." Paper prepared for LASA International Congress.

Municipalidad de San Joaquín. 1993. "Plan de Desarrollo Comunal: 1994-1996" and "Diagnostico Comunal San Joaquín, Región Metropolitana."

O'Donnell, Guillermo and Philippe Schmitter. 1986. *Transitions from Authoritarian Rule*. Baltimore: Johns Hopkins University Press.

Offe, Claus. 1990. "Reflections on the Institutional Self-Transformation of Movement Politics: A Tentative Stage Model," in Russell Dalton and Manfred Kuechler (eds.), *Challenging the Political Order*. Oxford University Press. Pp. 232-50.

Olea, Raquel. 1992. "La redemocratización; mujer, feminismo y política." *Revista de Crítica Cultural*. No. 5, year 3, July. Pp. 30-33.

Olson, Mancur. 1971. *The Logic of Collective Action: Public Goods and the Theory of Groups*. Cambridge: Harvard University Press.

Oxhorn, Philip. 1995. *Organizing Civil Society: The Popular Sectors and the Struggle for Democracy in Chile*. University Park: Pennsylvania State University Press.

_____. 1994. "Understanding Political Change After Authoritarian Rule: The Popular Sectors and Chile's New Democratic Regime." *Journal of Latin American Studies*. October. Pp. 737-760.

_____. 1992. "Where Did All of the Protestors Go? Popular Mobilization, Transition to Democracy and the New Democratic Regime in Chile." Ph.D. Dissertation, Harvard University.

Paley, Julia. 1994. "Knowledge and Urban Social Movements in Post-Dictatorship Chile." Ph.D. Dissertation, Harvard University.

Paramio, Ludolfo. 1991. Democracia y Movimientos Sociales en América Latina." *Revista de Ciencias Sociales*. No. 1. América Latina, Hoy. Pp. 13-18.

Pastor, Robert A. "How to Reinforce Democracy in the Americas: Seven Proposals," in Robert Pastor (ed.), *Democracy in the Americas*. Pp. 139-155.

Pateman, Carole. 1989. *The Disorder of Women: Democracy, Feminism and Political Theory*. Cambridge: Polity Press.

_____. 1970. *Participation and Democratic Theory*. Cambridge: Cambridge University Press.

Pérez-Díaz, Victor M. 1993. *The Return of Civil Society: The Emergence of Democratic Spain.* Cambridge, Massachusetts: Harvard University Press.

Petras, James. 1970. *Politics and Social Forces in Chilean Development.* Berkeley: University of California Press.

Petras, James and Fernando Ignacio Leiva. 1994. "Social Movements and Electoral Politics." *Democracy and Poverty in Chile: the Limites to Electoral Politics.* Boulder: Westview Press.

Phillips, Anne. 1992. "Must Feminists Give Up on Liberal Democracy?" *Political Studies,* Vol. XL. Pp. 68-82

Pozo, Hernán. 1986. "Partidos políticos y organizaciones poblacionales I: Una reflección problematica." Documento de Trabajo, no. 309. Santiago, Chile: FLACSO.

Pridham, Geoffrey. 1993. *Securing Democracy: political parties and democratic consolidation in southern Europe.* London: Routledge.

PROSAN. 1992. "Organizándonos para elaborar proyectos." Santiago, Chile: PROSAN. Pamphlet.

Quiñones, Luis. 1994. "La organización y representación de los pobres." Documento de Trabajo. Santiago, Chile: PET.

Raczynski, Dagmar. 1991. "Descentralización y Políticas Sociales: Lecciones de la Experiencia Chilena y Tareas Pendientes." Colección Estudios, no. 31. Santiago, Chile: CIEPLAN.

Raczynski, Dagmar and Claudia Serrano (eds.). 1992. *Políticas Sociales, Mujeres y Gobierno Local.* Santiago, Chile: CIEPLAN.

Rai, Shirin M. And Geraldine Lievesley (eds.). 1996. *Women and the State: International Perspectives.* London: Taylor & Francis.

Randall, Vicky and Georgina Waylen (eds.). 1998. *Gender, politics and the state.* London: Routledge.

Razeto, Luís. 1994. "Sobre el futuro de los talleres y microempresas." *Economía & Trabajo.* Año II, no. 3. Santiago, Chile: PET. Pp. 49-76.

Razeto, Luís, et al. 1990. *Las Organizaciones Economicas Populares, 1973-1990.* Santiago, Chile: PET.

Revilla, Marisa. 1991. "Chile. Actores Populares en la Protesta Nacional, 1983-84." *Revista de Ciencias Sociales.* No. 1. América Latina, Hoy. Pp. 61-66.

Ritter, Alan and Julia Conaway Bondanella (eds.). 1988. *Rousseau's Political Writings.* New York: W.W. Norton.

Roberts, Kenneth Morgan. 1997. "Beyond Romanticism: Social Movements and the Study of Political Change in Latin America." *Latin American Research Review*. Vol. 32, no. 2. Pp. 137-151.

———. 1992. "In Search of a New Identity: Dictatorship, Democracy, and the Evolution of the Left in Chile and Peru." Ph.D. Dissertation, Stanford University.

Rojas Hernandez, Jorge. 1992. "Desafíos estructurales del movimiento sindical chileno en el proceso de transición a la democracia," in Echeverría and Rojas (eds.), *Añoranzas, Suenos, Realidades*. Santiago, Chile: Ediciones SUR.

Rosenthal, Naomi and Michael Schwartz. 1990. "Spontaneity and Democracy in Social Movements," in Bert Klandersman (ed.), *Organizing for Change: Social Movement Organizations in Europe and the United States*. International Social Movement Research, Vol. 2. Greenwich, CT: JAI. Pp. 33-59.

Rousseau, J.J. 1762/1968. *The Social Contract*. New York: Penguin Books.

Santana Rodriquez, Pedro. 1991. "Gobiernos locales, descentralización y democracia." Paper presented at meeting of the Inter-American Foundation in Tepoztlán, Mexico.

Sartori, Giovanni. 1962. *Democratic Theory*. Detroit: Wayne State University Press.

Schild, Verónica. 1992. "Struggling for Citizenship in Chile: A 'Resurrection' of Civil Society?" Paper presented at LASA International Congress.

———. 1991. "Disordering Differences: Women and the 'Popular' Movement in Latin America (The Case of Santiago)." Paper presented at LASA International Congress.

Schmitter, Philippe C. 1998. "Contemporary Democratization: The Prospects for Women." In Jane Jacquette and Sharon Wolchik (eds.), *Women and Democracy*. Baltimore: Johns Hopkins University Press.

———. 1993a. "Organized Interests and Democratic Consolidation in Southern Europe." Unpublished manuscript, Stanford University.

———. 1993b. "Some Propositions about Civil Society and the Consolidation of Democracy." Paper presented at conference on "Reconfiguring State and Society." University of California, Berkeley.

———. 1985. "The Consolidation of Political Democracy in Southern Europe." MS, European University Institute.

Schmitter, Philippe and Wolfgang Streck. 1985. *Private Interest Government: Beyond Market and State*. Sage Press.

Schneider, Cathy. 1995. *Shantytown Protest in Pinochet's Chile.* Philadelphia: Temple University Press.

———. 1989. "Mobilization at the Grassroots: Shantytowns and Resistance in Authoritarian Chile." Ph.D. dissertation, Cornell University.

Scott, Joan W., Cora Kaplan, Debra Keates (eds.). 1997. *Transitions, Environments, Translations: Feminisms in International Politics.* New York: Routledge.

Sigmund, Paul E. 1977. *The Overthrow of Allende and the Politics of Chile, 1964-1976.* Pittsburgh: University of Pittsburgh Press.

Scott, W. Richard. 1992. *Organizations: Rational, Natural and Open Systems.* Englewood Cliffs, New Jersey: Prentice Hall. Third Edition.

Silva Donoso, María de la Luz. 1987. *La participación política de la mujer en Chile: las organizationes de mujeres.* Buenos Aires: Fundación Friedrich Naumann.

Sørensen, Georg. 1993. *Democracy and Democratization: Processes and Prospects in a Changing World.* Boulder: Westview Press.

Stallings, Barbara. 1978. *Class Conflict and Economic Development in Chile, 1958-1973.* Stanford: Stanford University Press.

Stepan, Alfred. 1988. *Rethinking Military Politics: Brazil and the Southern Cone.* Princeton: Princeton University Press.

Stephen, Lynn. 1997. *Women and Social Movements in Latin Ameica: Power from Below.* Austin: University of Texas Press.

Taller. 1989. "Las Organizaciones de Subsistencia en la Transición a la Democracia." Serie Trabajo y Democracia, 3. Santiago: Editorial Tiempo Nuevo, S.A.

Tarrow, Sidney. 1994. *Power in Movement: Social Movements, Collective Action and Politics.* Cambridge: Cambridge University Press.

———. 1991. "Struggle Politics and Reform: Collective Action, Social Movements, and Cycles of Protest." Cornell Studies and International Affairs Western Societies Paper. Occasional Paper #21, second edition. Center for International Studies, Cornell University.

Thompson, James D. 1967. *Organizations in Action.* New York: McGraw-Hill Book Company.

Touraine, Alain. 1989. "An Introduction to the Study of Social Movements." *Social Research* 52:4. Pp. 749-788.

———. 1988. *La Parole et le Sang.* Paris: Editions Odile Jacob.

_____. 1987. "Actores sociales y sistemas políticos en América Latina."
PREALC.

UNICEF, MIDEPLAN, FOSIS. 1993. *Solidaridad: La construcción social de un anhelo*. MIDEPLAN: Santiago.

Urmeneta, Roberto. 1990. "Las organizaciones economicas populares."
Cartilla de Capacitacion y Difusion No. 42. Santiago: PET.

Urzúa Valenzuela, Germán. 1988. *Los Partidos Políticos Chilenos: las fuerzas políticas*. Santiago, Chile: Ediar-Conosur Ltda.

Valdés, Teresa E. 1994. "Movimiento de Mujres u Producción de Conocimientos de Género: Chile, 1978-1989," in Magdalena León (ed.), *Mujeres y Participación Política Avances y desafíos en América Latina*. Bogota: TM Editores. Pp. 291-317.

Valdés, Teresa et. al. 1989. "Centros de Madres 1973-1989, Sólo disciplinamiento?" Documento de Trabajo no. 416. Santiago, Chile: FLACSO.

Valdés, Teresa and Enrique Gomáriz. 1992. "Mujeres latinoamericanas en cifras: avance de investigación Chile." Documento de Trabajo. Santiago, Chile: FLACSO.

Valdés, Teresa and Marisa Weinstein. 1993a. *Mujeres que sueñan: las organizaciones de pobladoras en Chile 1973-1989*. Santiago, Chile: FLACSO.

_____. 1993b. *Organizaciones de Pobladoras y Construcción Democrática en Chile*. Santiago, Chile: FLACSO.

Valdés, Teresa, and Marisa Weinstein, Marcela Diaz, and Sandra Palestro. 1993. "Mujer popular y Estado: informe de investigación." Documento de Trabajo. Santiago, Chile: FLACSO.

Valenzuela, Arturo. 1978. *The Breakdown of Democratic Regimes: Chile*. Baltimore: The Johns Hopkins University Press.

Valenzuela, J. Samuel. 1990. "Democratic Consolidation in Post-Transitional Settings: Notion, Process, and Facilitating Conditions. Working Paper #150. December.

Vanderschueren, Franz. 1971. "Significado político de las juntas de vecinos en las poblaciones de Santiago." *Revista Latinoamericana de estudios urbanos regionales*. Volume 2. June. Pp. 67-90.

Verba, Sidney, Norman H. Nie, and Jae-on Kim. 1978. *Participation and Political Equality*. London: Cambridge University Press.

Wachendorfer, Achim. 1990. "Sindicalismo latinoamericano, un futuro incierto." *Nueva Sociedad*. November-December. Caracas, Venezuela.

Waylen, Georgina. 1996. "Democratization, Feminism and the State in Chile: The Establishment of SERNAM," in Shirin M. Rai and Geraldine Lievesley (eds.), *Women and the State International Perspecitives.* Pennsylvaina: Taylor & Francis Inc. Pp. 103-117.

Whelan, James R. 1989. *Out of the Ashes: Life, Death and Transfiguration of Democracy in Chile,* 1833-1988. Washington, D.C.: Regnery Gateway.

Whiting Jr., Van R. 1984. *Political Mobilization and the Breakdown of Democracy in Chile.* Monograph series, vol. 1, no. 1. Brown University.

Wilson, James Q. 1973. *Political Organization.* New York: Basic Books.

Zald, Mayer N. and Roberta Ash. 1966. "Social Movement Organizations: Growth, Decay and Change." *Social Forces.* No. 44. Pp. 327-41.

Zald, Mayer N. and Patricia Denton. 1963. "From Evangelism to General Service: The Transformation of the YMCA." *Administrative Science Quarterly.* Vol. 8, no. 2. September. Pp. 214-234.

Zald, Mayer N. and John D. McCarthy (eds.). 1987. *Social Movements in an Organizational Society.* New Brunswick, NJ: Transaction Books.

Zolberg, Aristide. 1972. "Moments of Madness." *Politics and Society,* No. 2. Pp. 183-207.

NEWSPAPERS AND MAGAZINES

La Cuarta
La Epoca
La Hoja
Hoy
Marea Alta
Mensaje
El Mercurio
La Segunda

INTERVIEWS
As cited within text.

Index

For Product Safety Concerns and Information please contact our EU
representative GPSR@taylorandfrancis.com
Taylor & Francis Verlag GmbH, Kaufingerstraße 24, 80331 München, Germany